J-B-T21 y

Taylor, Zachary

'84- 1850

D0848975

Free Public Library
Atlantic City, N. J.

OLD ROUGH AND READY

Zachary Taylor

Born: November 24, 1784
Died: July 9, 1850

An aristocrat who never lost the common touch, a fighting general who often attacked war and a political amateur who became the 12th President of the United States, Zachary Taylor was one of the decisive figures in shaping our country's destiny. Descended from one of Virginia's first families, Taylor spent his childhood in the untamed Kentucky wilderness. As a young officer in the War of 1812, his scorn for the trappings of military rank and his unwillingness to ask anything of his men he would not do himself won him the affection of his troops and victories that brightened the darkest days of the American cause. In the years that followed, his reputation as a soldier and leader grew, and during the Mexican War, "Old Rough and Ready's" brilliance and courage in battle led to his nomination for the Presidency. His victory was the triumphant peak of a career cut short by his death in office.

BOOKS BY BOB AND JAN YOUNG

ACROSS THE TRACKS
54-40 OR FIGHT! The Story of the Oregon Territory
FORGED IN SILVER: The Story of the Comstock Lode
THE 49'ERS: The Story of the California Gold Rush
FRONTIER SCIENTIST: Clarence King
GOOD-BYE, AMIGOS
THE LAST EMPEROR: The Story of Mexico's Fight for
  Freedom
OLD ROUGH AND READY: Zachary Taylor
PLANT DETECTIVE: David Douglas
SEVEN FACES WEST
SUNDAY DREAMER

Old Rough and and Ready

Zachary Taylor

BOB and JAN YOUNG

Julian Messner • New York

Free Public Library
Atlantic City, N. J.

Published simultaneously in the United States and Canada by
Julian Messner, a division of Simon & Schuster, Inc.,
1 West 39 Street, New York, N.Y. 10018. All rights reserved.

Copyright, ©, 1970 by Bob and Jan Young

Printed in the United States of America

ISBN 0 671-32319-9   Cloth Trade
       671-32320-2   MCE

Library of Congress Catalog Card No. 74-123169

Contents

3.50

May71

210080

Contents

One

THE DARK AND BLOODY GROUND

Chief Dragging Canoe described Kentucky as "bloody ground, dark and difficult to settle," but to young Zachary Taylor the chilling description was merely a challenge. So far as he was concerned, his home, not far from Louisville, was the greatest place in the world to grow up in. He didn't ever want to leave.

For untold centuries, Kentucky had been a neutral zone between the warring northern and southern Indian tribes. Later it was the scene of fierce battles between Indians and the frontiersmen. It was still wild and dangerous when the Taylors left their Hare Forest home not far from the roaring Rapidan River and settled, in 1785, near the Falls of the Ohio River. No one ever thought of going to bed without being certain that all windows and doors were barricaded, and that primed and loaded muskets were near at hand to resist an Indian attack. Zach was only a few months old when they arrived but his father, Lieut. Col. Richard Taylor, saw that the two older sons, Hancock and William, were conscious of the dangers which surrounded them, and all of the nine Taylor children were encouraged to be both fearless and resourceful. Colonel Taylor's personal courage and skill was an excellent example for the youngsters to emulate.

Colonel Taylor had the same example set before him, hav-

7

ing been born in a family of fighters, pioneers and gentlemen, all extremely sensitive of their honor. This lineage produced two American Presidents—James Madison, the fourth
President, and Zachary Taylor, the 12th.

The first Taylor to arrive in the colonies was James, who
sailed from Carlisle, England, during the mid-1600s. He settled down with his wife, Frances, and became a landowner,
lawyer and public official. Descendants increased the Taylor
family substance and influence; most of them became military men of distinction. Richard Taylor, father of the future
President, was born in 1744 in Virginia. With an older
brother, Hancock, he began exploring and trading in the wilderness areas between Pittsburg and New Orleans. Theirs
was the first commercial venture in these uncharted territories. Richard spent a year alone with the Choctaw, Chicka-
saw and Creek Indians, seeing for the first time some of the
"dark and bloody ground" which captured his fancy. It was
probably then that Taylor decided where he would establish
his plantation.

With the explosion of the American Revolution, Richard
Taylor enlisted in the First Virginia Regiment as a lieutenant, and fought with great distinction at White Plains, Monmouth and Brandywine, finally retiring from the army as a
colonel after five years of service. He was 36 when he married Sarah Dabney Strother, during August of 1779. She was
about 18 years old at the time, a belle from a cultured, respected family. She had been educated in private schools or
by tutors. The six-foot-two-inch, blue-eyed colonel and his
diminutive blonde wife made a handsome pair to face the
perils of the wilderness and marriage for the rest of their
long, productive lives.

The Taylors had lived about five years at their stately
mansion in Hare Forest, Orange County, Virginia, and their
family had increased with their first two sons, Hancock and
William. Mrs. Taylor was pregnant with a third son when

her husband decided to claim the 6,000 acres of Kentucky land which was available as a war bonus. He chose the land which he had seen many years before.

With their sons, numerous servants and field hands (the euphemistic titles for slaves) the Taylors started for their new home. Mrs. Taylor became ill because of the strain of the venture and required rest at the home of a relative at Montebello, Orange County. It was there on November 24, 1784, that their third son, Zachary, was born. He was named after a deceased grandfather. "Little Zach," as he was called, spent his first seven months in Orange County.

It was not feasible to move either mother or infant son, so Colonel Taylor hurried on to Kentucky, where he began constructing a log home and clearing the land of timber and cane brake. The plantation was named Springfield.

The site was on the Muddy Fork of the Beargrass Creek, about six miles northeast of Louisville, a settlement chartered in May 1, 1780, which now boasted of "one hundred inhabitants who had cleared and cultivated garden spots around their humble cabins. . . . All else was primeval forest, with panthers, bears, wolves and wildcats. The familiar sound of the Falls of the Ohio River was sometimes disturbed by the yell of the savage, but all else bore the solemn silence of the deep, dark woods all around. . . ." Louisville had a future, Taylor believed, because it offered safe anchorage for the riverboats. He remained happy with his decision for the rest of his life, about forty-five years.

The first years at the plantation were those of hard work, danger and some sadness. A son was born there but died in infancy. There is no exact record of either the date or the name of the infant. It is believed that he was named, posthumously, Richard, and was born after Zachary but before George. It is this discrepancy in the family records which has most genealogies stating that Little Zach was the third child of nine, even though only eight are usually listed.

There were Hancock, William, Zachary, the infant Richard, George, Elizabeth, John, Joseph and Emily.

There was no place in the Taylor family for timid, fearful children, but Colonel Taylor was a loving, protective father. Because of incipient Indian dangers, he cautioned the exuberant brood of children against straying too far from home. As late as 1795, a public fund was maintained to pay Kentuckians for Indian scalps taken in the vicinity of Louisville. Despite the potential dangers, Zach and the other Taylor children gloried in the wild beauty which surrounded their home. The rolling plain was dotted with maples, cottonwoods, oaks and cedars, many of great size. Game abounded too—deer, wild turkey, ruffed grouse, bear and rabbit. And there was always good fishing for black bass, bream or catfish. Excitement lurked everywhere; panthers and vicious cane-brake rattlesnakes were constant dangers.

As he gained his inches, Zach developed into a thickset lad, with short legs carrying his puncheon-shaped body. His skin was fair and often sunburned. Zach's hair was dark, and his eyes were penetrating and gray, often twinkling in suppressed humor. All of the Taylor children had a family resemblance, although their inherited features were somewhat more plain than handsome.

When Colonel Taylor chose the wilderness, he forsook the buckled shoes, ruffled shirts and other fine clothes of the landed Virginians. They were replaced with homespun or buckskin garments. His example was followed by the Taylor boys. Zach, for example, was often clad in a buckskin shirt, blue jeans, homemade moccasins and a coonskin cap. It was the style of Daniel Boone, who lived not far away. Zach wanted to emulate either his father or Boone, and so did many of his young friends. One was George Crogham, who lived two miles away. His mother was a sister of the famed George Rogers Clark, who also lived with the Croghams. Often Zach listened to the tales of General Clark. He also

visited the plantation called Soldier's Retreat, owned by his
father's friend Colonel Richard Anderson. Living there was
the eccentric Mrs. Chenoweth, who amused the children by
suddenly whipping off her bonnet to display a completely
bald head, which had been "peeled like an onion by the Indians' bluntest scalping knife."

With such experiences to mold their young minds, Zach
and most of his friends looked forward to carving careers on
the frontiers, overseeing plantations and living a life surrounded by family and friends.

While Zach's parents agreed in part with their children's
ambitions, they wanted the youngsters to gain an education.
Colonel and Mrs. Taylor were both well educated and qualified to provide fundamental tutoring, but they realized their
shortcomings. With neighbors, all of whom had large families, they hired Elisha Ayres to teach the young people.
Ayres was an itinerant Connecticut schoolmaster whose pen-
chant to wander prevented a stable teaching situation.
Ayres's approach to education appealed to Zach and the others. It was in keeping with Ayres's observation: "The Kentuckians were then a warlike and chivalrous people who
often engaged in offensive and defensive skirmishes with the
Indians. A number of them [Indians] were known to be in
the woods not far distant from the schoolhouse, and on one
occasion, one of them was shot wearing a British uniform. . . ."

Even more important to the frontier-oriented youngsters
was Ayres's ability to obtain the services of Lew Wetzel,
whose wilderness exploits were legendary. From him Zach
learned how to reload a musket while running at full speed,
a feat which once saved Wetzel's life when he was being
pursued by three Indians. To master the skill, Zach spent
hours running and loading, giving up only when he was either successful or exhausted. Though Zach probably spent
more time outdoors using a musket than learning to write or

doing sums, Mr. Ayres's assessment of Zach's abilities as a
student was: "quick in learning and still patient in study."

Dogmatic schooling didn't interest Zach as much as the
books he read about military heroes, the craft of politics or
adventure. These subjects were often dinner-table topics in-
stigated by Zach's father who maintained that war was simply an overt extension of politics. All of the Taylor youngsters were enthralled with the often-told tales of fighting
and adventure which their father had experienced. Most of
Zach's games were based on warfare.

The seeds of romantic adventure planted in Zach's mind
by others flourished when he attended a Louisville academy
where Kean O'Hara was schoolmaster. O'Hara was an Irish-
man of wit and culture who had left his native land at the
outbreak of the 1798 revolution. Zach attended O'Hara's
school, though the number of years of schooling Zach had
is not certain. His later writing demonstrated wit, force
and dignity, although it did not always have the grace and
good spelling of a well-educated person.

During these early years, Zach and his brothers helped or
supervised such activities as clearing fields, felling trees, removing stumps, plowing, planting and harvesting. But any
tradition that Zach was born in a log cabin, or that he was
ever raised as anyone except a well-to-do planter's son, is
false. The great house at Springfield had been built as soon
as possible. It was a two-and-a-half-story brick structure
trimmed with pristine white, and it stood at the center of
the 400-acre parcel called "The Home Place." The Taylors
were affluent, since the Colonel owned more than 10,000
acres, most of it planted to tobacco, hemp or other cash-
money crops.

The mansion had huge doors which opened off each end
of the structure; an exit opened from the wide hallways
which ran north and south through the entire dwelling on
the ground floor. On the east side there were two high-ceil-

inged, paneled rooms, brightened by the sun, which flooded through two tall windows, and by huge fireplaces. Sturdy furniture, all of it made by the carpenters whom Taylor included among his slaves, was tastefully placed throughout the house. On the other side of the hall were other rooms, including the main dining hall. Cooking was done in a cabin outside the main house. After the Taylor family finally moved into the big house, the log cabin which had first accommodated them was moved and made into quarters for some of the field hands and servants.

A winding staircase led to the four bedrooms on the second floor. Zach's room was paneled with walnut and included a small fireplace and, best of all, a secret compartment above the closet that could be opened only by twisting one of the clothes hangers. Off Zach's bedroom was a porch, connected to the grounds by a narrow stairway, a feature which made the various war games even more interesting. A wide driveway circled the house. It was bordered with tall cedars, some of which were planted by Zach, who took an enduring interest in both the house and the area surrounding it. The entire grounds were landscaped with lawn, shrubbery and assorted trees, giving the mansion a gracious and secure air. Security was ensured, because the Colonel insisted that the surrounding area be kept clear so that any approach could be observed at a distance.

As Colonel Taylor prospered, other relatives purchased property in the general area, and the mansion at Springfield often rang with the laughter of many children and adults. Dinners, generous in quantity though not lavish in nature, were frequently given. Zach and his brothers occasionally provided the main dishes for these dinners by killing deer, wild turkey or grouse. Available to all were fine wines, usually port or sherry, and the gentlemen had the thin cheroots to smoke following the dinners. Many of these cigars were products of the tobacco grown in the Kentucky area.

These were happy moments in the activity in Springfield and in the life of Zach. In later years Zach often wrote of his regret that he could no longer be a part of the feasting, the spirited talk and the customary dances of trotting jigs or pigeonwings.

The Taylors' interests weren't confined to the home, and Zach profited by his father's interest in public affairs, an activity which the Colonel considered to be a citizen's solemn obligation. He served in several capacities, including justice of the peace and Collector of the Port at Louisville, the latter job being abolished when the French flag was lowered in 1803 following the Louisiana Purchase. Loss of the modest income was of trifling concern to the Taylors, who by now were among the largest land-owners and slaveholders in the area.

Zach liked to visit the burgeoning village of Louisville, which by 1804 boasted nearly 800 residents. Though its growth and increasing importance were due largely to its river trade along the Ohio and shipments of tobacco, its affluence didn't rest on grog ships or similar industry. Fineries of all sorts were available in Louisville shops, and the Taylors were frequent purchasers.

Zach was reluctant to leave home, though he wanted to make a career in the army. His father agreed, but his mother tried to make him stay at Springfield. Zach's older brother, William, was a second lieutenant in the artillery. He had seen no action, nor had he received any advancement, but his enthusiasm for his military career encouraged Zach. A combination of world events, however, shaped his final decision.

There was the threat of war in the air. Since the purchase of the Louisiana Territory from France in 1803, the United States and Spain had been haggling intermittently over the location of the boundary between this newly acquired territory and the Spanish-owned colony of Mexico.

Even more threatening was the worsening relationship between United States and Great Britain. France, an ally of the United States during the American Revolution, had been going through a period of upheaval since 1789. The French Revolution and the overthrow of the monarchy had been followed by war with most of France's neighbors, leading to the rise of Napoleon I, who, by 1805, had elevated himself from the elective office of First Consul to Emperor and seemed bent on the conquest of all Europe. At first the United States tried to maintain an attitude of neutrality in this conflict between France and Great Britain, but the stopping of American ships and forcible seizure of British crewmen for service in the British navy was stirring up a war fever in the States. Adding to the unrest was the increased fighting along the United States' expanding frontiers between American settlers and Indian tribes loyal to the British. In 1807 military excitement was further elevated by the attack of the British ship *Leopard* on the American vessel *Chesapeake*. Congress reacted to this incident by tripling the size of the army from its former limit of 3,000 men.

One of the new units activated was the Seventh Infantry, and Zach submitted a request for a commission in the unit. His father, probably through his relationship to President James Madison, arranged to have the petition immediately considered by Congress. Zach Taylor was one of 26 Kentuckians recommended to the War Department because the selections, Congressmen averred, were "to prefer the Sons of ancient settlers, who had distinguished themselves in the Defense of the Country or had suffered & withstood the inconveniences & Dangers of an early settlement therein. . . ." The phrasing couldn't have fit Colonel Taylor and his son Zachary any better if the plea had been written specifically for them.

Zachary Taylor was appointed a first lieutenant of the Seventh Regiment in the United States Infantry on May 3,

1808. He was probably as well qualified as any other man mustered into service at the time in view of his education, frontier training and background—perhaps better than most.

It was a month before he received the official notification, and Zach responded immediately, as befitted a newly appointed officer,

Louisville, Ky., June 6th, 1808

Sir,

I received your letter of the 4th of May in which you informed me that I was appointed a firs [sic] Lieutenant in the seventh regiment of Infantry in the service of the United States which appointment I doo [sic] accept.

I am Sir with great respect

your Obt. Servt

Zachary Taylor

The Honrl H. Dearborn S. at War

Curiously, one of the officers with whom Zachary Taylor would have a great deal of contention and association was commissioned at the same time. He was Winfield Scott, an officer who was later tagged with the sobriquet of "Old Fuss and Feathers." Scott was a man of extreme aristocratic inclinations, and he referred to his fellow officers as "coarse and ignorant" or, at best, "decayed gentlemen." But since they all held the same rank and drew the same pay ($30 a month plus $12 subsistence allowance) Taylor considered himself and others to be Scott's equal, and paid little attention to his caustic comments. Like his father before him, Zachary Taylor was proud of the uniform he wore. In Zach's instance it was a blue single-breasted knee-length coat with a collar which reached to the tip of his ear, blue pantaloons, white leather waist belts, a leather duty cap and black boots.

Because of a delay in the mails, combined with the fact that the Seventh Infantry was not fully organized, it was several months before Lieutenant Taylor received any spe-

cific orders to duty. In the interim, his older brother William
had been killed in an Indian attack at Fort Pickering some-
time during June, 1808.

Lieutenant Taylor was ordered to recruiting duty in
Mason County as his first assignment. He went to Washington, Kentucky, where he found only one officer, no recruits
and no further orders. Taylor immediately moved the headquarters (which included only a regimental drum and fife)
to Maysville, located on the Ohio River, where Taylor admitted: "I am rather badly off here on the score of society."

Taylor was modestly successful in recruiting but was
happy to be relieved of the routine, onerous duty in early
spring of 1809, when he was ordered to join his regiment at
New Orleans. He took a number of his rookies with him to
strengthen the Seventh Infantry which might be a key unit
in the defense of New Orleans. It was expected that the
British would attack there to shut off communications along
the Mississippi.

In command of the area was Gen. James Wilkinson, an
ambitious commander more interested in political intrigue
than in the welfare of his men. He stationed his men in a
swampy area about thirteen miles from New Orleans, a vir-
tual pest hole because yellow fever stalked the land. Taylor's
men, who had just experienced one of the coldest winters on
record, suffered heavily because New Orleans was undergo-
ing a heat wave the worst in 20 years. Despite the climatic
conditions, work went ahead on the fortifications.

Men, bone-tired from the day's work, got little refreshing
sleep because of the swarming mosquitoes which kept them
awake. With their lowered resistance, the soldiers fell prey
to diseases of all sorts. Sanitation was almost nonexistent, or
simply an attraction to vermin or germ carriers of every
sort. Food, supplied by corrupt contractors, was often fouled
when received or, even if it was wholesome, became contaminated in the kitchens. At best, it was poorly prepared.

". . . Attempts at burial were pitiful. Interred higgledy-piggledy in shallow graves, the protruding arms and legs of the deceased took the place of missing markers in reminding the living of the fate that might be theirs," historian Holman Hamilton wrote.

And there were many who followed these men to the grave. Nearly half of the 2,000 men died, deserted or were discharged because of chronic debilities.

Lieutenant Taylor was stricken with the fever, and the illness was compounded with dysentery. He wasted away until he was as thin as a rake and his ribs protruded like those on a cheap parasol. Taylor, with his chosen career in jeopardy, was depressed; but he felt much better when he was given an official furlough for rest and recuperation. On the way back to Springfield, Taylor considered the future. He was disappointed with the first experiences, but even more determined to recuperate, study military strategy and procedure and become as good an officer as he could.

His father and mother stood on the wide porch of their home when he rode up. Colonel Taylor saluted his son, and Zach returned the salute and grasped his father's hand in an affectionate gesture. Zach's mother ran to him and threw her arms about the ailing man. Together they walked into the mansion.

Zach looked back for a moment, scanning the grass spiked with the same trees he remembered climbing as a youngster. He smiled broadly.

"It is good to be home again," Zachary Taylor said, his voice tinged with emotion.

Two

DEFENSE OF
FORT HARRISON

Despite his disabilities, Zach Taylor was much too energetic to stay in bed long, though he did continue to rest while he studied military subjects to improve his skill as an officer. As his strength returned, Taylor began to take rides into Louisville. He fished and hunted, and spent many of his evenings attending dinners and social affairs. It was at one of these parties, given by Mrs. Samuel Chew, that Zach Taylor renewed his friendship with the lovely Miss Margaret (Peggy) Mackall Smith of Maryland. The slender Miss Smith was a member of a wealthy and prominent Maryland family and had been well educated in exclusive finishing schools, both in the United States and in Europe.

Miss Smith apparently had been as much impressed with the stocky young officer as Taylor had been with her. Their friendship quickly ripened into love, and they were married in the Taylor home at Springfield on June 21, 1810. He was 25 years old and his bride 21. Their marriage would last 40 years and 18 days. As a wedding present, Colonel Taylor gave them 324 acres of prime land near the mouth of Beargrass Creek. There Zach and Peggy built a home, and there she would return to give birth to five of their six children.

Lieutenant Taylor remained on inactive military status for almost a year. He took his bride with him when he was or-

dered to command Fort Pickering, just below the present
site of Memphis, Tennessee. It was located on the border of
the Mississippi Territory, high on a bluff. Taylor assumed
command with mixed emotions. As they mounted the 120
log steps which led to the fort, Taylor saw traces of blood on
each step. It was here that his brother William had been
killed just a year before. But the fort now offered little challenge, because the Indian danger had been largely elimi-
nated. Taylor continued intensive study of military matters,
and was commissioned to the rank of captain. His wife returned to Springfield to await the birth of their first child.
The infant, Ann Margaret Mackall Taylor, was born on April
9, 1811. Mrs. Taylor was still at Springfield when Captain
Taylor was ordered to Fort Knox, situated on the Wabash
River just above Vincennes. It was the nominal seat of military government for the Indiana Territory. Taylor faced a
chaotic situation in the new command. The former commandant, Capt. Thornton Posey, had fought a duel with a subordinate officer, Lieut. Jesse Jennings, and killed him. Posey
then deserted. None of the remaining officers had qualities
of command, and Taylor was sent to right matters at Fort
Knox. His command included elements of the Seventh Infantry, which was operating in concert with the Fourth
Frontier Infantry to support Gen. William Henry Harrison.
The troops were fighting the great Indian leader Tecumseh,
who had gone on the warpath when the Americans broke
the Treaty of Greenville and moved to take more Indian
land.

Taylor's skillful management of the fort was observed by
General Harrison, who wrote to the War Department after
Taylor had been in command for a few weeks:

". . . To all of these qualities which are esteemed for an
amiable man, he appears to have united those which form a
good officer. In the short time he has been commander

[Taylor] has rendered Fort Knox defensible—before, it resembled anything but a place of defense. . . ."

Taylor expected that his troops would be called out from the Fort to begin what was hoped to be the final attack on Tecumseh. He knew that Tecumseh and his brother, who was called The Prophet, had been assembling their braves to fight for land which the white men had wrongfully seized from them. General Harrison had attempted negotiation but failed. He was convinced that decisive military measures had to be taken if the territory was ever to be secured. The previous "pacification" which Gen. "Mad Anthony" Wayne had effected in the Northwest Territory following the Battle of Fallen Timbers was obviously undone. The disputed areas were again as hazardous as they had been during the days when General Wayne went to subdue them.

President Madison was interested in settling the matter without further bloodshed, and the Indians indicated some willingness to talk. But in the field, General Harrison was taking matters into his own hands, preparing for what became the Battle of Tippecanoe. (Tippecanoe was a tributary of the Wabash River, which rises near what is now the Ohio-Indiana line.)

While still in command of Fort Knox, Taylor was given what he referred to as "a very handsome command." As General Harrison prepared for the campaign which started from Vincennes on September 26, 1811, Taylor had 910 men in his command. But just as the attack was launched, Captain Taylor received urgent orders to report to New York military headquarters. Taylor was required to testify to the faulty command procedures and the dire conditions which prevailed in the New Orleans area. With his testimony given, Taylor was able to leave New York and hurry back to his command. But the decisive battles had been successfully fought, and The Prophet's villages destroyed. The Indians' spirit had not been crushed, however, and depredations continued.

Captain Taylor had another concern. His wife and infant daughter were still at Springfield when one of America's great earthquakes occurred—on December 16, 1811, in the Tennessee-Kentucky area. The earth breathed sulfurous fumes, and the ground groaned with cataclysmic movements and reversed the course of the Mississippi River long enough to form Reelfoot Lake, 14 miles long. Temblors continued for weeks, and dust draped the sky for months. With the lack of fast communication, Taylor could not know his wife and child were safe.

There was another military assignment for Taylor—urgent because of the growing concern with the military activities of the British and the Indians, who had apparently formed an alliance against the Americans. Taylor was assigned to command Fort Harrison, an outpost which stood three miles above Terre Haute. When war was finally declared on June 18, 1812, Captain Taylor anticipated active military service.

The first American military adventure ended in utter failure. General Hull attempted an invasion into Canada, but his entire command surrendered on August 16. The British army, supported by the Pottawattomies and Ottawas, swarmed into the American territory and captured all of the forts above Wabash. An assault was mounted against Taylor's pitifully small garrison at Fort Harrison. Somehow Taylor learned of the offensive against the Americans and, unaware of Hull's disastrous defeat, wrote to his commander stating that Tecumseh was preparing to attack during the next full moon.

"They all agree," Taylor wrote about his intelligence reports, "that his present force is much larger than it was last fall, and one of them says that [Tecumseh] expects a large

reinforcement, . . . It is possible that his first attempt will
be against this post or Vincennes. . . ."

Taylor refrained from saying that his own situation was
perilous; ammunition stores were low, and many of his men
were ill with fever. His forces were actually so depleted that
Taylor could mount no more than six enlisted men and two
commissioned officers for guard. It became Taylor's custom
to omit information of danger about himself or his command. He seemed supremely confident in being able to overcome the obstacles which confronted him. His confidence
was not always justified, but his courage was never ques-
tioned.

Though Fort Harrison had become a strategic point in the
war, the garrison itself didn't physically amount to much.
The fort was only 150 feet square, its palisades constructed
of oak and honey-locust logs. The fort stood about 30 feet
above a sharp bend of the Wabash River, and its blockhouses overlooked both the river and the four-foot deep
trenches which flanked three sides of the fort.

Tension mounted as the men awaited an attack, but it
failed to materialize at once. Despite fever and other ill-
nesses, the soldiers completed their duties as best they
could. Suddenly the waiting was over. Four shots thundered
in the evening quiet of September 3. The alarm was
sounded. Taylor refused to panic, even though he knew
there were two young frontiersmen beyond the safety of the
fort. "It isn't prudent", he stated, "to send a patrol that late
in the evening. The danger was too great."

There was no commissioned officer to whom Taylor
thought he could safely delegate full authority. And there
were still only a fraction of the roster who could report for
duty and bear arms. Taylor could not afford to lose any of
them. Next day, a patrol was sent to recover the bodies of
the young men who were found "each shot with two balls,

scalped and cut in the most shocking manner." They were buried within the fort, and the security watches were increased. An attack now appeared imminent. Taylor cautioned the guards to be extremely vigilant, then retired early. He had just recovered from another attack of fever and "was not able to be up much through the night."

Just before midnight of September 4, the sound of gunfire roused Taylor. He jumped from bed to discover that the Indians not only were attacking under the cover of musket fire, but had already set fire to the southwest blockhouse, a building in which the fort's rations were stored. "The guns had begun smartly from both sides," Taylor wrote later.

"Get the buckets. Draw water from the well!" Taylor yelled. But the men were discouragingly slow. One woman, Julia Lambert, was equal to the need. She lowered herself to the bottom of the well, then helped hoist brimming buckets to the top. The fire raged on undiminished, and played havoc with the stores of whiskey. A blazing sheet of flame raced toward the roof to the blockhouse. "As the night was very dark, and in spite of every exertion we could not extinguish the fire," Taylor said.

Flames seemed to engulf the blockhouse and threatened the main storehouse. Unless something was done, Taylor realized, the Indians would be able to scamper through the burned hole and overwhelm both soldiers and civilians. The cries of the women and children mingled with the frenzied shrieks of the maddened Indians.

"I can assure you that my feelings were very unpleasant," Taylor related afterwards. There were only 10 to 15 men fully able to respond to Taylor's commands, and "two of the stoutest men in the fort jumped the pickets and left us."

In his subsequent report to General Harrison, Taylor wrote: "My presence of mind didn't desert me. I saw that by throwing off part of the roof that joined the blockhouse which was on fire, and keeping the end perfectly wet, the whole row of buildings might be saved, and leave only an entrance of 18 or 20 feet for the Indians to enter after the house was consumed; and that a temporary breastwork might be erected to prevent their entering even there. I convinced the men that this could be accomplished, and it appeared to inspire them with new life, and never did men act with more firmness and desperation. . . ."

Taylor ordered Post Surgeon William Clark to oversee the civilians and disabled. Taylor took close command of the men as they continued to defend the fort against the several hundred Indians who were attacking the garrison. Taylor's plan worked, even though the fire continued to flare during the night and required the full efforts of all who were able to control it. The Indians pressed the attack. One soldier, Pvt. Bill Cowan, yelled, "I killed an Indian." He was so elated with his success that he failed to duck and fell back with a musket ball in his head. Two others became casualties when they mounted the roof of the blockhouse. But the others were able to construct the breastwork before morning. By that time, the soldiers' musket fire began taking deadly effect and the Indians withdrew beyond range. The fort was saved.

Taylor realized that the Indians might be regrouping to mount another assault on the fort. He waited for two days. Rations now consisted of little more than green corn. Taylor called for volunteers to sneak past the Indians and obtain help from Vincennes. Two men paddled down the river, and their remains were returned a few hours later by the Indians.

Taylor then sent a sergeant and a private, ordering them to move through the woods at night, not along the open trails. "Although neither of them has ever been to Vincennes by land," Taylor said, "nor did they know anything about the country; but I was in hopes they could reach Vincennes in safety. . . ."

With the messengers gone, there was nothing to do but wait, watch and hope. Rations were reduced even further. Because the Indians hemmed in the fort, there was no chance to forage for food. The fort could conceivably be starved out, even if the Indians didn't decide to make another attack and overwhelm the pitifully weak garrison of hungry and ill defenders. Taylor estimated they couldn't last more than 48 hours more. After that, he planned to make a desperate break-out, keeping the women and children within a hollow square of men after leaving the protection of the fort. Taylor ordered preparations be made for the sally. The people were assembled, instructions given and sentries ordered to make a final visual survey of the Indian positions. Even before they had mounted the palisades, gunfire echoed across the river. The staccato of noise increased in tempo and a lookout yelled:

"Americans. American troops. We're saved."

Other men jumped to the rifle ports or peekholes to confirm the happy news. It was true. Col. William Russell was marching at the head of 1,200 men sent to rescue the beleaguered fort. They arrived on September 16, not a minute too soon. Colonel Russell reported that they had met with no resistance, and that supply wagons had been dispatched to the fort even before they were aware of the desperate situation.

Russell was impressed with Taylor's defense of the fort and his conduct during the seige. Russell wrote General Harrison about it, referring to "the firm and almost unparalleled defense of Fort Harrison by Capt. Z. Taylor."

Harrison relayed that praise to President Madison, adding to it with his comment the defense was "one bright ray amid the gloom of incompetency which has been shown in so many places."

President Madison was impressed with their comments, and Taylor was brevetted to the rank of major as of September 5, 1812. (A brevet is a temporary rank given in place of a medal.) The President recognized that the defense of Fort Harrison was not merely a frontier skirmish, but one of military significance because it was a key point to secure a large area which would otherwise lay open to both Indian and British attack. Whether Taylor knew or considered this when he undertook the valiant defense is not known and makes scant difference. He had successfully seized on the first opportunity to distinguish himself after five years of service. Taylor's feat was widely lauded and circulated through favorable articles in the *Niles Register*. Taylor gained national prominence as a result of this publicity. Years later, even when other battles were fresher in the public memory, Taylor was often referred to as that "brave young man who had beaten off the red men at Fort Harrison."

The war was moving ahead on many fronts, both on land and sea. Major Taylor's determined stand on the east bank of the Wabash signified the first American military victory in the War of 1812. Taylor was detached from command of the fort and became an aide to Maj. Gen. Samuel Hopkins, commander of all troops in the Wabash Valley and the Illinois Territory, including 2,000 of Taylor's fellow Kentuckians. There was little glory in this campaign, which was directed against Peoria and the Kickapoo Town along the banks of the Illinois River. Lacking army regulars, the professional soldiers who compose an effective fighting unit, Hopkins had difficulty with obedience among the men. Besides, the expedition was poorly equipped and guided. Provisions ran low, and guides got lost. Morale was so low that when General Hopkins asked for five volunteers, not one man stepped forward. The situation became impossible and unmanageable. Rather than march into disaster, Hopkins decided to return to Fort Harrison—even though nothing had been accomplished. Major Taylor led a few patrols into the Indian villages which were found along the Illinois and Wabash rivers. Once, when 51 men deserted in the fury of a fight, Taylor's patrol almost dissolved in disaster, but he managed to extricate the others, leaving only one American dead. But as the men moved along, the Indians would suddenly appear, attack and then disappear into the forests after they had inflicted cruel losses. It was a war of nerves, and the Americans suffered terribly.

"After reconnoitering sufficiently, we returned to base," General Hopkins wrote, "and found the ice so accumulated as to alarm us for the return of the supply boats. I had fully intended to have spent one more week in endeavoring to find Indian camps; but shoeless, shortless state of the troops, now clad in the remnants of their summer uniforms; a river full of ice; the hills covered with snow"—a condition which forced them to quickstep out of the Indian Territory. Again Taylor's conduct was commended by Hopkins for "the prompt and effectual support given by Major Taylor." Hopkins then added that "the firm and almost unparalleled defense of Fort Harrison by Major Z. Taylor has raised for him a fabric character not to be effaced by my eulogy."

Perhaps as a reward, Major Taylor was assigned to superintend recruiting services in the territories of Indiana and Illinois. It was with some relief that he was later assigned to duties in the Missouri Territory, but he was forced to leave Mrs. Taylor behind when the British pressed their attacks. At length his command was changed to Fort Knox, and it was there, on March 6, 1814, that their second daughter, Sarah Knox Taylor, was born.

Three

THE SON IN LAW?

Troops stationed in the Missouri Territory were in an exposed position, since it was believed that the British might try to sweep down from the north toward St. Louis, capturing the American forts as they advanced. Gen. Ben Howard, who was in over-all command, planned to move up the Mississippi to offset the expected British move. At the last moment Howard fell ill of fever, and the command of the troop movement devolved upon Major Taylor, with orders which said, in part: "Major Taylor will ascend the Mississippi as high as the Indian Vilages [sic] at the mouth of Rock River . . . and destroy the Vilages. He will after effecting or failing to effect the object at that place drop down to the Demoine [sic] and erect a fort which must be maintained until further orders can be sent. . . ."

Taylor realized that he had been given a formidable task. He would face Black Hawk, leader of both the Sac and Fox Indians, a wily and determined fighter who was being generously supplied with weapons, ammunition and even artillery by the British. Black Hawk, born in 1767, had watched his tribal home, situated along the Rock River at a place called Watch Tower, burned at the order of Gen. George Rogers Clark. Black Hawk swore that he would oppose any white settlement along the upper Mississippi. Black Hawk sent the Indian women and children to the rear, then chose a place where he planned to fight the Americans. With him were 1,500 Sac and Fox Indians, one large bore cannon and a keg of rum.

On August 22, 1814, Taylor set out from Fort Independence with 430 militiamen and rangers and a few cannon and supplies, all contained in eight boats. Taylor was in the lead keelboat. "We set out with hearts elated and sails filled," Capt. James Callaway jotted down in his diary for that day.

Moving upstream was very difficult. The soldiers were often forced to wade and pull the heavily laden boats. When there was no wind, Taylor ordered that oars be used, often until "a number of the men were ready to feint with fateuge." Many of the men fell ill with measles, and one soldier died. For two weeks, they struggled upstream. No Indians had been seen, but Taylor kept a white flag flying from his masthead to assure the Indians that they meant no harm.

It was near dusk on Sunday, September 4, when they reached the mouth of the Rock River. A great number of Indians were assembled and waiting for them there. At the sight of the soldiers some of the Indians moved farther upstream, while others crossed the river below Taylor's boats. Taylor realized the danger of being surrounded. He moved quickly toward Rock Island, which was near the middle of the river and would provide them cover not only from the Indians but from the storm, which was mounting to a hurricane strength. The men slept on their weapons that night, many of them in the boats. There was no attack by the Indians.

Before daybreak, the Indians began an attack, their first musket and cannon assault killing one man and damaging several of the keelboats. Taylor ordered one unit to fight off the Indians who had landed on the island. Capt. Sam Whiteside commanded the cannon fire from the small swivel guns mounted on the boats against both the Indians and their canoes. Capt. Nelson Rector attacked the Indians from another quarter to scatter their fire. But the Indians returned the fire with a six-pound cannon directed by Lieut. Duncan Graham of the English Indian Department. The British had also reinforced the Indians with two more three-pound cannons, which were brought to bear on Taylor's men.

Taylor decided that their position was no longer tenable, and for the only time in his long military career, he ordered a retreat.

"Take to the boats, men. We'll float downstream, below the rapids," Taylor yelled to his men.

Though Taylor had failed to destroy any Indian villages as ordered, he knew that fulfillment of the order was contingent upon the situation. It was most important that a fort be started to give the Americans firm foothold in the area. Taylor jumped into a boat and waved his arm in a signal for the men to move out. As he did, there was a splintering crash. A cannonball smashed through the boat inches from where Taylor stood. The hold was above the waterline, but Taylor threw a line to another boat to secure them if the boat was swamped while moving downstream.

The Indians continued firing at the retreating Americans, but most of them scattered when Taylor ordered a round of grapeshot fired from the swivel guns. Black Hawk's men continued to harass Taylor as they floated. About two miles below the Indian camp, Taylor ordered a landing and defenses set up. His casualties had been amazingly slight: Paul Harpole was dead and ten others had been wounded. Boats were beached so they could provide cover and be mended. Emplacements were dug to shield the men. When the Sacs and Foxes appeared and saw Taylor's men ready to fight on land, they fled "in as great hurry as they had followed us," Taylor wrote.

With the enemy driven off and their boats repaired, the

Americans moved on. Near the mouth of the Des Moines
River, work began on Fort Johnson. The site was located on
a high river bank, near the present site of Warsaw, Illinois,
and was named after Col. Richard Johnson, the officer cred-
ited with killing Tecumseh. The work was well underway
when a courier arrived with the news that Gen. Ben Howard was dead and Taylor was needed to assume command
of the Missouri Territory military department. Before leaving for the St. Louis headquarters, Taylor put Captain Callaway in command and assured him that ample supplies and
men would be sent to him and that work on the fort would
be expedited.

In a short time, Taylor was superseded in the command
by Col. William Russell. He then took an expedition up the
Missouri to strengthen a threatened outpost. Before leaving,
Captain Callaway arrived in St. Louis. He had burned and
abandoned Fort Johnson, complaining that the expected
men and supplies hadn't arrive. In Taylor's opinion, Callaway had abandoned his obligation and given another advantage to Black Hawk, who ultimately would have to be put
down. At the time Taylor speculated whether he would
have the chance to fight Black Hawk, or if this failure to
complete a mission would reflect on his military career. Taylor vowed never to retreat again, nor trust a job to anyone
else when he could or should do it himself.

Taylor made one more excursion up the Mississippi and
the Missouri to inspect small settlements which were being
threatened by the Indians. After that, he sat out the rest of
the War of 1812 and several months thereafter in a minor
command at Vincennes.

The war was formally concluded with the Treaty of
Ghent on December 24, 1814. On January 2, 1815, Taylor received official notification that he had been advanced to the
permanent rank of major and was assigned to the 26th Infantry, which was stationed on the northeastern frontier.

The news came as a relief. Taylor had been fretful as he watched his friend George Crogham advance to the rank of lieutenant colonel. Winfield Scott was now a brigadier general. Taylor complained, and his Congressman Stephen Ormsby wrote the Secretary of War: "Major Zachy Taylor, the son of Colonel Richd Taylor of Kentucky, who Gallantly defended Fort Harrison complains that he had been neglected and overlooked, while his junior officers had been promoted."

The Kentucky Congressmen bluntly pointed out that Taylor was well connected to high officials who were "warm supporters of the Govt" and suggested that something be done. Confirmation of Taylor's promotion followed, but the elation was of short duration. With the onset of peace, the Army shrank. Taylor's promotion had been approved after the war was over, and therefore was not valid, according to a War Department interpretation. Taylor was offered the permanent rank of captain, if he wanted to remain in the peacetime army. The army was to be reduced from 50,000 to 10,000; only 39 of the 216 field-grade officers (majors and above) would be retained, and only 450 in the 2,055 lower ranks. President Madison took a hand to prevent Taylor's reduction in rank, noting that Taylor had been the first officer to be brevetted and that his advancement had been made because of bravery.

"The defense of Fort Harrison that led to it, though in an obscure theatre of war," the President wrote to Secretary of War Dallas, "has probably not been exceeded in brilliancy by any affair that has occurred. The circumstances of it put to the severest trial the military qualities of the commanding officer, and it appeared that the result was conspicuously favorable to him. . . ."

Despite this high praise from President Madison and the admission by the General Staff that sheer carelessness and haste had been responsible for overlooking additional advancements for Taylor, his case was considered unalterable since the confirmation of permanent rank had not come until after the war was over. There would be no exceptions.

Angered at the injustice of the decision, Taylor resigned his Army commission and was given an honorable discharge on June 15, 1815. His brother Joe also was discharged when the army reductions were effected.

Although he was piqued at the treatment, Taylor realized that he was happy to come home again and "make a crop of corn." For almost a year, Taylor lived with his family as a farmer.

"I can assure you," Taylor later wrote a cousin, "that I do not regret the change of calling or the course I have pursued. . . ."

With a number of field hands available to him, Taylor's work wasn't too demanding, even though the methods were primitive. Wheat was threshed by being trampled by mules; corn was shelled by rubbing ears on roughened boards; and new land was cleared rather than restoring the old with the use of fertilizer.

Taylor spent much of his leisure time talking politics with friends, especially John J. Crittenden, a Kentucky assemblyman who later became U.S. Senator and Governor of Kentucky. Though the Whig political party had not been organized at that time, Taylor and Crittenden were of the same social philosophy, ostensibly Whig. They were alarmed at the concentration of federal power, the tariffs imposed during the war and the reconstruction programs which were under way.

With the spirited talk, the refreshments of cooling drinks and fine cigars, the days slipped by happily. But President Madison, for one, wasn't content to let Taylor's military skills lay fallow. He was recommissioned as a major in the Third Infantry on May 17, 1816. His brother Joe was reinstated as a second lieutenant in artillery at the same time.

Mrs. Taylor was not able to travel with her husband because she was pregnant, this time with Octavia Pannil Taylor, who was born on August 16, 1816, at the family home. Major Taylor was far north by that time.

The United States was engaged in a program of fort building to protect trade in the Great Lakes area, and to police the smuggling activities there. Major Taylor was assigned to command of Fort Howard at Green Bay, an arm of Lake Michigan. There were about 300 soldiers of the Third Infantry, along with French-Canadian voyageurs and their squaws, settled within the Fort's jurisdiction. Taylor acted decisively in crushing the smuggling through the use of Winnebagoes as spies. Though he won commendation for his work and was well liked and respected by his men, Taylor wasn't happy with the command.

In the fall of 1818, after nearly two years of his dreary duty, Taylor was sent to Louisville for recruiting duty. Being near home, Taylor was able to oversee the plantation work and to live with his family. Another daughter, Margaret Smith Taylor, was born on July 27, 1819.

After the isolation of Fort Howard, the bustle of Louisville, now a city of 8,000 people, seemed exciting to Taylor. There was time for leisurely dinners and lots of good talk with friends. President James Monroe, elected in 1816, took office in what one newspaper described as "The Era of Good Feelings," a phrase which was both apt and contagious. Major Taylor was delighted when the President visited Kentucky and he was designated as one of the official escorts. Taylor himself was still considered a hero, as indicated by an observor who wrote:

President James Monroe has arrived and departed. He was received with due public honors, as the papers will inform you. Yesterday, the President breakfasted with us, in company with Gen. Jackson and that hero whose cool, determined and successful courage has never been rivalled in an-

cient or modern times, who so bravely defended Fort Harrison, Major Zachary Taylor. . . ."

Though there was no apparent connection with the official
visit or the impression which Taylor made on the President,
not long afterwards he was commissioned to lieutenant colonel. He was assigned to the Fourth Infantry then transferred
to the Eighth Infantry.

During February of 1820, Taylor and his family traveled
down the Ohio and Mississippi rivers to Bayou Sara, where
he settled his wife and children with Mrs. Taylor's sister,
Mrs. Chew. The Taylors wanted to establish a home somewhere in the Mississippi Valley, though they weren't sure
just where. No immediate decision could be made because
of Taylor's uncertain military assignments.

It was a tragic trip. All of the Taylors fell prey to the yellow fever. Octavia died on July 8, and Margaret died on October 22. For some time, doctors despaired of Mrs. Taylor's
life but she survived. The ravages of that illness, however,
weakened her so much that she was a semi-invalid for the
rest of her life. After that tragic personal loss, Taylor began
to talk of "when I quit the army," a speculation which he
never realized.

Lieut. Col. Taylor was now assigned to men of the Eighth
Infantry busy with the construction of the Jackson Road, a
military route about 200 miles long. The Taylors were all reunited at the Bay St. Louis, and lived there while Taylor
went on to construct what later became Fort Jesup, a site on
the Louisiana frontier, during 1822.

Busy as he was with army duties, Taylor purchased a
plantation not far from Baton Rouge, on which cotton was
planted. His management was interrupted when he was
again ordered to recruiting duty during 1824 in Louisville.
The duty was vital because of the massive desertions from
the Army, almost 10 per cent of the 8,000-man army.
Though Taylor wanted to stay near his plantation, his new

assignment would be near Springfield, where two more children were born—Mary Elizabeth Taylor on April 20, 1824, and the last child, Richard, on January 27, 1826.

Because of his military assignments, Taylor had never been able to vote in any presidential election. But he was interested in politics and particularly concerned with the four-way presidential contest in 1824, largely because his friend Henry Clay was one of the candidates. The votes were scattered among the contestants, and none of the four got a majority. The election had to be decided in the House of Representatives. Although Andy Jackson had received 99 electoral votes and John Quincy Adams only 84, Adams was elected when Clay supporters favored him. Jackson followers cried "foul" to no avail. Clay was named Secretary of State, and Taylor learned a few of the machinations which comprise professional politics.

During the next few years Taylor, now a full colonel, served in various administrative posts and became increasingly interested in the art of politics. He was back in Baton Rouge when the 1828 presidential campaign began.

Taylor had become a friend and admirer of Andy Jackson and was particularly distressed by the venomous attacks made on both Jackson and his wife, who was excoriated because she occasionally smoked a pipe. Mrs. Jackson, as Mrs. Taylor would be later, was opposed to her husband's seeking political office but had to suffer the slings and arrows which went with national office. Taylor was denied any chance to take part because his assignment was shifted to command of Fort Snelling, located near the present site of St. Paul, not far from the confluence of the Mississippi and Minnesota rivers.

Fort Snelling, built in 1829, was an imposing stone structure. It was one of the most remote American outposts and was militarily supported both by Fort Crawford, at the mouth of the Wisconsin, and by Fort Armstrong, where the

Rock River enters the Mississippi. Fort Snelling was the center of unrest among the Fox and Sac Indians, the tribes which Black Hawk led. There were no overt attacks by the Indians, and relations were maintained through Indian agents. Taylor was assigned to that post in the fort area. He was notably sympathetic to the Indians and managed the affairs peaceably.

Colonel Taylor was commandant at Fort Snelling when his 18-year-old daughter, Ann, fell in love with the post surgeon, Dr. Robert Crooke Wood, and he with her. Ann was a slender young lady with brown hair and gray eyes. Dr. Wood was a tall, slim man who was considered handsome. He had graduated from Columbia Medical School in 1821 and was 30 years old at the time of their marriage on September 20, 1829. They had four children, including two sons who fought for the Confederacy.

Confirmation of Taylor's permanent rank as colonel finally arrived, and he was transferred to Fort Crawford to command the First Infantry. Colonel Taylor was now 47 years old and considered an excellent officer with extensive military experience. Upon arriving at Fort Crawford, Taylor ordered the immediate improvement of the bastion, which was occasionally inundated when the river rose. With his frontier experience and the confidence which comes with years and skills, Taylor handled his men knowingly and casually. He often took time to drill troops himself, or was close at hand if subordinate officers did the task.

Shortly after arriving at Fort Crawford, Taylor ordered a full-dress inspection. Among the new recruits in the command was a German youth who understood very little English. Often he misinterpreted orders. Taylor told the young man to step forward from the line. He stood still. Taylor snapped the order again, and still the rookie stood in place. Enraged because he thought the soldier was being disobedient, Taylor strode up and grabbed his head by the ears and shook it violently. The German lad, not understanding the order or the action, pulled his head free and slammed his fist into Taylor's face. Taylor fell to the ground, dazed. Other officers moved to shoot the youth, for striking an officer under such conditions was mutiny. But one man explained that the young man could not understand. Taylor laughed, then waved the others away as he dusted himself.

"Put away those guns and don't do anything," Colonel Taylor said. "That man will make a good soldier. He fights when there is a need."

Taylor might dismiss insubordination among some of his troops, but fractiousness at home was quite a different matter. He had approved of the marriage of his daughter Ann to Dr. Woods, but when Sarah Knox Taylor was being courted by Lieut. Jefferson Davis, a recent graduate from West Point, Colonel Taylor objected strenuously. There were at least two reasons, according to the Colonel's reasoning.

Taylor, like many officers who had risen through the ranks, was suspicious and uncomfortable with the well-trained but often officious West Point graduates. While Davis was a fine officer, he had further alienated Colonel Taylor by becoming embroiled in a fracas during an Indian wedding ceremony. Davis insisted on dancing a waltz step with an Indian girl while music for quadrilles was being played, so that he could hold her in his arms. At length the girl's brother objected to Davis' actions, even though they were harmless. A fight followed in which Davis drew a pistol and the Indian a knife. It was necessary for Colonel Taylor to step between the men and stop the fight.

Taylor and Davis differed about other matters, and Taylor finally forbade Davis to even call at the Taylor house for any reason.

"I will be damned if another daughter of mine shall marry

into the army," Colonel Taylor stormed. "I know enough of the family life of officers. I scarcely know my own children, or they me."

Lieutenant Davis, a fiery Southerner born in Kentucky, was so upset by what he thought to be a completely arbitrary decision that he considered calling the Colonel out for a duel. Fortunately, he was dissuaded. When military operations began not long afterwards, Taylor made Davis one of his staff aides because he lacked any other suitably qualified officers.

His infatuated daughter, who was usually called Knox, consoled her father but refused to break off an engagement with Davis.

"The time will come," Knox said, "when you will see as I do all of his rare qualities."

Four

THE BLACK HAWK WAR

Seeds of the Black Hawk War had been sown several years before the conflict actually erupted. During the spring of 1832. By treatment similar to that which had been accorded other Indian tribes, the Sac and Fox Indians had been pushed back from their tribal lands by the advancing white settlers. Finally, Black Hawk's followers decided to make a fight for their lands.

Black Hawk, or Makataimeshekiakiak, was 64 years old— ancient by most fighting standards. But he had the wisdom of age and of having fought with the British in the War of 1812, and he was implacable in his resistance to the forward movement of the Americans. In 1804 a treaty had been signed by the United States and the Sac and Fox Indians which ceded all of the lands east of the Mississippi River to the white men. The Indians were to have the area between the Wisconsin and Illinois rivers as their tribal grounds, so long as they remained in the public domain. The seat of the Indian tribal government was established along the Rock River, about three miles from its mouth. There the Indians established their villages, planted fields and buried their ancestors. It seemed to have aura of permanence.

Following the 1812 war, settlers began moving into the area to take up parcels of the lush farmland, which sus-

41

tained fine crops of corn, beans and squash. Black Hawk protested about the settlers' moving in, and when his pleas were ignored, the Indian Chief threatened to kill the settlers. The settlers immediately appealed to Governor John Reynolds of Illinois for help. In turn, he asked the army to move in and quiet the situation. Little attention was paid to the justice of Black Hawk's claims, or the fact that Indian villages had been burned while the Indians had been absent on a hunting trip. Gen. Edmund Gaines, late in June of 1831, sent about 3,000 soldiers into Black Hawk's province to impress the Indians and protect the settlers.

Under the unrelenting pressure of army force, Black Hawk led all of his people across the Mississippi, where they joined other Indians who had been forced to move. A few days later, Black Hawk, summoning all of his Indian courage, took about 25 of his subchiefs to meet with army officers. As a result of that conference, Black Hawk signed an agreement never to return to the east side of the Mississippi River. Thus it appeared in 1831 that the Indian troubles had been settled. Gaines withdrew most of his troops, leaving two companies of infantrymen at Fort Armstrong.

"Had the garrison of Fort Armstrong been re-enforced as it could & ought to have been, with three or four companies," Taylor wrote later about the handling of the affairs, "there would have been no indian [sic] war."

During April of 1832, Black Hawk agreed to the requests of his tribe, who insisted that they had a right to return to their tribal lands across the river, despite the treaty. Black Hawk, six feet tall, slight almost to the point of emaciation, with piercing eyes and carved features, led the crossing. His tribe took all of their belongings, indicating they were moving peacefully but permanently. That would never do, army officials said, and the alarm of Indian danger was sounded.

Troops were mustered from several states, including one company of Illinois Volunteers which was commanded by

Capt. Abraham Lincoln. In all, there were several thousand soldiers, regular army and militiamen, sent into the area. Colonel Taylor, under the command of Generals Atkinson and Whiteside, moved into the Rock River area, intent upon the defeat of Black Hawk and his followers.

"We set out in pursuit of the enemy," Taylor wrote, "with six companies of the 4th and 6th infantry, amounting to about 320 rank and file in addition to the militia."

Since Taylor moved by water in order to bring up both men and supplies, other units were in the skirmish area before Taylor arrived. The Americans had been defeated by the wily old Black Hawk in their first encounter.

Seeing the array of men and weapons coming up the river, Black Hawk sent out what appeared to be a truce party. Ostensibly these Indian braves would ask to return to the west of the Mississippi. Three Indians went ahead, and five waited at a safe distance to the rear, high on a prominence. They approached Major Isaiah Stillman, whose militiamen were bivouacked at the lead of Old Man's Creek. The untrained troops, thinking that this might be an Indian trick, got panicky and shot at the flag bearers. One of the Indians was killed. The rest fled.

Black Hawk seized the opportunity to fall on the disorganized and frightened Americans. With a detachment of his braves, Black Hawk swooped down on Stillman's troops, killing 12 men in the first attack. Then confusion and terror consumed the men, and "they became panic struck, & fled in the most shameful manner that every [sic] troops were known to do, in this or any other country, there were some seven or eight killed in the pursuit, & it is probable had it not been just at night when the attack was made on the Indians, that a very large proportion of the whites have been killed, the cover of night enabled them to get off," says Taylor's scorching account of the skirmish which actually touched off the Black Hawk War.

"That disgraceful affair of Stillman ought not to have occurred. . . . The officer should have prevented it. . . .
That attack made on the indians brought on the war. . . .
Had the regular troops overtaken them, at any rate in con-
junction with the Militia men then in the field, before any
blood had been shed, they would have been removed back
to the West side of the Mississippi, without a gun being
fired. . . ." It may have been Taylor who gave the battle the
derisive name of "Stillman's Run," in deference to the frightened troops who straggled into Dixon's Ferry, Taylor's command post. General Atkinson was busy elsewhere with Indian depredations, and Taylor was left in full command at
the outpost trading center which had been built by John
Dixon. There was a 90-foot-long barracks where Dixon's
wife fed the transients, who then were ferried across the
river by her husband.

Troops from many states were stationed at Dixon's Ferry.
Capt. Abe Lincoln ate and chatted with Lieut. Jeff Davis.
The men got along famously. At the same table sat Albert S.
Johnson and Joseph E. Johnson, both of whom were to be-
come famous in the Civil War; Nat Boone, son of Daniel
Boone was there, along with William S. Hamilton, son of Al-
exander Hamilton.

Captain Lincoln, who re-enlisted as a private when his
company was mustered out, saw no close combat during the
war. But he got a taste of what was happening during a patrol. He found five soldiers who had been slain during an
ambush, and he recalled later: "Each of the dead men had a
round spot on the top of his head about as big as a dollar,
where the redskins had taken his scalp. . . . It was frightful,
grotesque. . . ."

Atkinson was engaged in operations against the Indians
some distance from Taylor's command headquarters. He was
gathering his men to form one arm of a pincer movement
against Black Hawk. But the green troops under his com-

mand had other ideas. The militiamen, comparable with the national guards, had been enlisted on the promise that they would not have to fight outside of their state. Rock River was considered the northwestern boundary. Taylor, however, had orders to "Pursue Black Hawk until he is captured." Taylor meant to carry out the orders.

Colonel Taylor showed his capacity for command when he spoke to the reluctant soldiers. "You are citizen-soldiers and some of you may later fill high offices, or even be president some day, but never unless you do your duty." It was prophetic that his audience included Abe Lincoln. The men asked for a brief time to discuss the matter among themselves. In a few minutes, Taylor spoke again:

"I have heard with much pleasure the views which several speakers have expressed of the independence and dignity of each private American citizen," Colonel Taylor began with deceptive mildness. "I feel that all of the gentlemen here are my equal in reality. I am persuaded that many of them will in a few years be my superiors and perhaps in the capacity of members of Congress, arbiters of the fortunes and reputations of humble servants of the Republic like myself. I expect to obey them as interpreters of the will of the people; and the best proof that I will obey them is now to observe these orders of those whom the people had already put in places of authority, to which many gentlemen around here justly aspire. In plain English, gentlemen, word has been passed on from Washington to follow Black Hawk and to take you with me as soldiers. I mean to do both. There are flatboats drawn up on the shore, and there are Uncle Sam's men drawn up behind you on the prairie. . . ."

The militiamen looked at each other, then at the boats and the troops with menacing muskets standing behind them. Someone remarked they had the law on their side, but another observed that the bayonets of the army regulars behind them was all the law that Colonel Taylor needed, and the men piled into the boats for further pursuit of Black Hawk. Others might fail to resolve their problems, but Taylor wasn't one of them.

More troops moved into the area, though not before more than 200 settlers had been killed by the marauding Indians. "You have no idea, nor can I describe the panic & distress produced by these murders," Taylor wrote to a friend in relating an Indian attack which killed all the members of three families, except for two young women who were carried off.

Even as the military pressure increased, Black Hawk fought a skillful delaying and rear-guard action. His ranks had been thinned during the weeks of desperate fighting; his rations were low and the noncombatants, women and children, whom he brought along with him slowed his mobility in fighting the American troops. Taylor saw that Black Hawk was being pushed into a *cul de sac* from which he would be unable to extricate himself. One force, operating under the command of Gen. James Henry and Col. Henry Dodge, encountered a large band of Indians along the Wisconsin River. Nearly 70 Indians were killed in the battle, with the loss of one American soldier. Despite the defeat, Lieut. Jeff Davis, who had taken part in the battle, believed the military tactics of Black Hawk were unexcelled.

". . . The most brilliant exhibition of military tactics I ever witnessed; had it been performed by a white man, it would have been immortalized as one of the most splendid achievements in all of military history," Davis later wrote.

The Black Hawk War was nearing an end. It would culminate at the Battle of Bad Axe, in which Taylor took part. Black Hawk's fighting strength was weakened by the battle of Wisconsin Heights. Hungry, wounded and tired, the Indians moved dispiritedly toward the mouth of the Bad Axe River, where it emptied into the Mississippi. But the American troops were tired too.

". . . After I may say a forced march of nearly thirty days, during which were suffered every privation and hardship common to our profession . . . we succeeded on the morning of August 2d inst. in overtaking the Indians on the bank of the Mississippi while in the act of crossing and preparing to cross about forty miles above Fort Crawford," Taylor later wrote.

The heavily armed steamboat *Warrior* was in the river ready to deal with the now almost helpless Indians. Three quick rounds of cannon fire cut a swath through the Indians, and 23 were killed in the first barrage. Night stopped the slaughter, but Black Hawk was being beseiged on every quarter. At dawn on the next day, the troops began to close in. Black Hawk took some of his men and stood in full view on riverbanks high above the camp. In this way, Black Hawk believed, the main body of the Indians could escape safely even though his own life might be forfeit.

"Born of desperation, this stratagem was brilliant. It almost worked," one military historian commented.

The American troops began to move toward Black Hawk, who was offering such a tempting target. Atkinson was moving forward on the right flank. Taylor and Dodge were advancing in the center, while General Henry protected the baggage and the rear of the troops. Chance favored Henry. His scouts located the main body of the Indians, who were covertly moving down the river, not upriver as Black Hawk wanted the Americans to believe. Henry ordered his troops to charge, and the close-quarter combat involved braves as well as women and children. For the Indians it was a Hobson's choice—death on land or death in the water—but there was no alternative except death.

Taylor's unit moved into the fray, taking part in the pursuit of the Indians. Taylor waded waist-deep through a broad slough to a willow-covered island. The men fired as they sloshed ahead. Taylor's troops drove all of the Indians from cover, then killed and captured them one by one.

As Black Hawk's people were being attacked by Taylor's

men, the *Warrior* had moved in from the riverside. An ulti-
matum was given to the Indians. They were given 15 minutes to get their women and children out of the area, then
the cannon would be turned on them. It was an appalling
demand. One poignant incident was recorded in the *Niles
Register*:

"A young squaw of about nineteen stood in the grass at a
short distance from our line, holding her little girl in her
arms, about four years old. While thus standing, apparently
unconcerned, a ball struck the right arm above the elbow
and shattered the bone, and passed into the breast of its
young mother, which instantly felled her to the ground. She
fell upon the child and confined it to the ground also. During the whole battle this babe was heard to groan and call
for relief, but none had come to afford it. When however, the
Indians had retreated from the spot and the battle subsided,
Lt. Robert Anderson . . . went to the spot and took from
under the dead mother her wounded daughter and brought
it to the place we had selected for surgical aid. It was soon
ascertained that its arm must come off, and the operation
was performed without drawing a tear or a shriek. . . . It
was brought to Praire du Chien, and we learn that it has
nearly recovered. . . ."

The massacre was complete within about three hours, and
the Black Hawk War was all but over—"killing, I presume
one hundred, & making fifty or sixty prisoners, besides de-
stroying a large portion of their baggage, & killing, & capturing a number of their horses with a loss on our own part of
some twenty-seven killed, & wounded; since which number
of prisoners has been picked up, mostly women & children
in attempting to recross the Mississippi to the west," Taylor
wrote in describing the final events.

Perhaps Taylor's account was modest, because many of
the Indians no doubt were shot and killed in places beyond
discovery, such as the Mississippi or Bad Axe rivers. Black

Hawk was captured shortly after the last battle and was taken first to Jefferson Barracks in St. Louis and then to Washington. Following his solemn promise to President Jackson to live in peace, Black Hawk was returned to his tribe and lived out his remaining years there, faithful to his word.

Aboard the *Warrior,* Colonel Taylor returned to Fort Crawford, arriving there on Saturday evening, August 4, 1832. His wife and daughter Knox were on hand to greet him, making a return from the war even more pleasant.

A few days later, Gen. Winfield Scott visited the fort. He had been delayed in reaching the fighting front because of an outbreak of Asiatic cholera among his men. An epidemic of the dreaded disease followed his arrival. The plague reached the Indian tribes and killed scores of them. Numerous desertions occurred as soldiers left trying to escape the peril.

Colonel Taylor, now assigned to the First Infantry, took full command of Fort Crawford and was once again safe and happy with his family. Taylor was vocal and bitter about the conduct of the war. He said, among other things, that the Black Hawk War was a classic ineptitude, costing 1,000 lives and $3,000,000, all of which had been needlessly squandered.

"There has been an error somewhere," Taylor observed. "But how or by whom it has been committed is not for me to say, & my only wish now is that we may profit by past blunders. . . ."

It was a charitable way in which to anticipate a period of peace and quiet, good for a man 47 years old, financially snug and with a handsome wife and a growing, happy family.

Five

THE SEMINOLE WAR

With the conclusion of the Black Hawk War and the assumption of the command at Fort Crawford, Colonel Taylor anticipated a period of peaceful routine. Not only had the Indians been put down, but Taylor managed to get Lieut. Jeff Davis assigned to escort Black Hawk to the Jefferson Barracks at St. Louis. His absence would mean an end to his courtship of Knox Taylor.

With his gradual promotions in rank, Colonel Taylor's military conduct softened. He was more relaxed and casual with his fellow officers, in his uniforms and in his handling of military duties. He appeared more at ease with the travelers who occasionally visited the isolated fort. Following a dinner, the Colonel served some of the fine-vintage wines which had been in the basement of the residence provided the commandant. Taylor drank sparingly, if at all. And he objected strenuously to intoxication. He approved the formation of the Fort Crawford Temperance Society, though he was not a zealous reformer among his troops, except where drinking interfered with performance of duties. Taylor encouraged the use of the post library, occasional dances and theatricals presented by soldiers of the garrison. He provided a large barracks building to be used as a theater, with the seats arranged in amphitheater fashion. The fort was spacious, enclosing a drill ground within the compound. The commandant's headquarters and hospital were adjacent to the main enclosure.

Taylor was disturbed again when he learned that his daughter Knox and Lieutenant Davis were still corresponding. Taylor thought that Knox had given up the young man when he had expressed his objection to their marriage. But since their romance had continued, Taylor realized that there would have to be a decision. Knox was firm in her engagement to Davis, writing to him regularly when he was assigned to Fort Gibson in Oklahoma. It had not been out of sight and out of mind, as Colonel Taylor hoped.

Colonel Taylor continued to thunder his opposition in tones which would have reduced his troops to silence, but his words had no effect on Knox. And Davis was equally determined. If the Colonel's only objection to their marriage was the fact that he was an army officer, Davis offered to resign immediately and seek another career. Colonel Taylor realized that he had been outgeneraled, but he was never one to retreat no matter the prospect of defeat. He had his own personal pride, as well as respect for the commandant's office to be considered and upheld. Taylor realized that he was fighting a losing battle when a relative invited Knox to visit her in Kentucky.

He knew it was female conspiracy against him. Secretly, Mrs. Taylor helped her daughter prepare a trousseau before she left Fort Crawford; but by avoiding any confrontation, everyone saved face. Colonel Taylor stood stiffly on the dock as he watched his pretty daughter standing on the rear deck, her hands clenched and her face streaked with tears, as the small boat sailed down river toward Louisville. It appeared to be a family impasse until Knox wrote a letter to her parents. In it, she said she had been married on June 17, 1835, in the presence of her sister, Ann, Dr. Wood and (Uncle) Hancock Taylor, who attested to the fact that she was of legal age and could be married without parental consent. Then she added:

. . . You will be surprised, no doubt, my dear mother, to hear of my being married so soon. When I wrote to you last I had no idea of leaving here until fall, but hearing the part of the country to which I am going is quite healthy, I have concluded to go down this summer and will leave here this afternoon at 4 o'clock; will be married as you advised in my bonnet and traveling dress. I am very much gratified that Sister Ann is here. At this time having one member of my family present, I shall not feel so entirely destitute of friends.

But you, dearest mother, I know will retain some feelings of affection for a child who has been so unfortunate as to form a connection without the consent of her parents, but who will always feel the deepest affection for them whatever may be their feelings toward her. Say to my dear father that I have received his kind and affectionate letter and thank him for the liberal supply of money sent me. . . .

The latter statement was most curious, not only because Taylor had written Knox, but because he had enclosed some money. Taylor was always a man to be conservative with money.

Lieutenant Davis made good on his statement to withdraw from the army. With his bride, Davis undertook to superintend his plantation, Brierfield, located about 20 miles from Vicksburg. It was an isolated, lonely place, but the newlyweds didn't mind. There were many field hands and servants. It seemed like an idyll, but it was star-crossed. Brierfield lay within the fever-ridden area, and the Taylors were concerned about their daughter's health. Davis agreed that they should leave Brierfield until the summer fever season was spent. They moved in with Davis' sister, who owned a Louisiana plantation, Locust Grove. But it was too late. Knox had been infected, and Jeff came down with the fever too; both fell ill at the time they moved. High fevers ravaged them, with Knox's condition becoming critical.

As Jeff Davis lay awake one night, he heard the wild love song which they had adopted as their own during the stolen courtship hours being sung in Knox's bedroom. Though desperately ill, Jeff jumped from bed and ran to his bride. Knox had fallen into a coma by that time, and she died on September 15, a little less than three months after her marriage.

Davis was plunged into gloom and withdrew from the world for eight years, leaving the management of his property to others. During his bereavement Davis read omniverously, perhaps formulating the plans which would lead him to the presidency of the Confederate States.

Years later, Davis was about to board a Mississippi riverboat when he met Taylor. The men faced each other for a tense moment as an icy, uncomfortable silence ensued. Taylor then smiled, offering his hand. Taylor realized, perhaps at that moment, that Davis had loved his daughter as deeply as he had. There was no reason for them to hate each other. They became good friends for the rest of their lives.

The years which Colonel Taylor spent as commandant of Fort Crawford were routine. Taylor was becoming increasingly aware of national and world events and the part that the American government was playing in them. There was restiveness among the residents of the Southern states because of the agitation against slaveholding. Free states pointed to the example of Great Britain, which had outlawed slavery throughout its realm in 1833. A royal payment of £20,000,000 was authorized by Parliament to pay off the bondage of about 700,000 slaves. Taylor, a slaveowner, wondered if such an issue would arise in the United States.

About another matter, American feelings were less divided. The threat of war with Spain had long since vanished, but the border with Mexico was still unsettled. Though Spain had assisted Great Britain in the defeat of

Napoleon, her days as a colonial power were over. Many of
her colonies in South America had used the temporary abdi-
cation of the Spanish king during the Napoleonic struggle as
an excuse to declare their independence. Mexico had become
independent in 1821. To help keep down Indian uprisings
on the northern frontier and act as a kind of buffer zone
against the United States' expansion, American settlers were
encouraged to take up Mexican land grants and citizenship
in Texas. The plan did not work. These new settlers continued to make New Orleans their trade center instead of Mexico City. Most were from the South and owned slaves. When
Mexico abolished slavery, they refused to follow suit. In
1836 the Mexican general Santa Anna led an army north to
bring them back in line. The Mexican victory at the Alamo
was followed by a crushing defeat at San Jacinto. Texas became an independent republic, and Santa Anna was shipped
home in disgrace.

Like most of his fellow citizens, Taylor's sympathies were
with the Texans. With the First Infantry he was ordered to
Fort Jesup near the Texas border, a garrison he had helped
construct. But before he could get under way, the orders
were countermanded and he and his battle-tested First Infantry were sent instead of Florida to fight the Seminole Indians. According to General Order 50, Taylor was to report
to Tampa Bay between October 10 and 15, 1837.

The Seminoles, led by their wily chief, Osceola, had baf-
fled the Army for 18 months, slipping through marsh, swamp
and cypress groves. The general staff was disgusted and
tired of being frustrated and made the fool. Thus began one
of the blackest chapters of man's treatment of man.

Shortly after his arrival in Florida, Taylor went to Fort
Drane. On his way, he stopped in a tavern at Newsmansville
to refresh himself. Taylor, who had started wearing casual
uniforms, was dressed in homespun pants and coat and wore
a straw hat typical of the farmers. He was seated at a table

when a young man entered the room. He was smartly attired in an army uniform which bore the gold bars of Second lieutenant. There was West Point apparent in his demeanor as he walked up to Taylor's table and sat down.

"Old man, how are the Seminoles doing now?" he asked Taylor. "I believe, sir," Taylor drawled, "they are giving considerable trouble to the officers—especially the young ones."

"That so? Well, it will be different from now on. I am an officer from West Point and am on my way to take charge. But then, that is no matter to you. Have a drink, old codger, and enjoy yourself here in the safety of the tavern."

Taylor suppressed a smile and thanked the young officer as he left the tavern.

A few days later the same rookie officer reported to the commanding officer of the First Infantry and found him to be the same "old codger" from the tavern. The young man was flustered, but Taylor only laughed at his discomfiture.

"Never mind, young man," Taylor said. "Just don't judge an officer by the kind of hat he wears."

The campaigns against the Seminoles proved to be, as one officer said, little more than a "forlorn hope." The elusive Seminoles, a breakaway tribe from the Creek Confederation, had resisted conquest for 20 years, and the army didn't seem much nearer victory when Taylor arrived in Florida.

The Seminoles, Taylor learned, had left the Confederation during the 18th century and, as fugitives themselves, welcomed all other Indians and runaway slaves from the Southern states. There was a benevolent association between slaves and the Seminoles. The Negroes usually preferred to live in the swampy recesses of the Everglades than return to their masters. Indians and slaves lived together in peace until 1817, when they were accused of a raid against the white settlements. The discipline by the army resulted in further Indian reprisals. In one case, 34 Americans were killed as a result of an ambush. Even General Jackson wasn't able to subdue the Seminoles permanently, though the Indians were temporarily contained in what was called the First Seminole War.

The Second Seminole War began after the Spanish sold Florida to the United States. The war cost $30,000,000 and 1,500 lives and became one of the ugliest, bloodiest episodes in American history. For Zachary Taylor, the war was a path to glory. It would earn him the brevet of a brigadier general and the sobriquet of "Old Rough and Ready," which characterized Taylor's willingness to undergo the privations of his men and always be ready to move out and fight the next day.

When Florida was acquired from Spain, the Seminole chiefs ceded all of their cultivated lands in the northern section of Florida and agreed to live in the area south of Tampa Bay. But when they realized what a poor bargain they had made, they refused to move southward and began to fight the settlers who were moving into Seminole territories. Sporadic fighting began again. Other bloody engagements erupted from the attempt to recover runaway slaves, but a full-scale war was averted for a time. Col. James Gadsden was sent to Florida in an effort to implement the government's policy of removing all Indians to the area west of the Mississippi River, in accord with the Indian Removal Bill of 1830. Gadsden was able to convince Micanopy, a fat, stupid old Seminole Chief, that it was to the benefit of the Indians if they moved. Micanopy agreed, provided the Seminoles were allowed to inspect the resettlement area. The Treaty of Fort Gibson, in 1833, was the result. Micanopy committed the tribes to leave within the next three years. When they refused, President Jackson sent troops into the area under the command of Gen. Duncan Clinch. That armed threat unified the Seminoles.

The Indians, led by a fiery young Seminole chief named Osceola, swooped down on a patrol near the Withlacoochee

River led by Maj. Francis Dade on December 28, 1835. Only three men survived from the 110 who took part in the fight. The Seminoles then killed five others at isolated areas.

"You have guns," Osceola wrote Clinch, "and so have we. You have powder and lead and so have we. You have men, and so have we. Your men will fight and so will ours, till the last drop of Seminole blood has moistened the dust of his hunting ground."

With this dramatically stark challenge the battle lines formed.

Clinch's military efforts were of little avail, because he could never pin down Osceola to fight a pitched battle along classic army theories. Gaines was not able to come to grips with the enemy either. Winfield Scott, who considered Gaines insane, was an utter failure too. Maj. Gen. Thomas S. Jesup was called in and he partially succeeded; but his triumph was attained through treachery rather than military tactics, stealth rather than strategy.

Jesup was unable to cope with Osceola's hit, run and hide tactics and was ridiculed in the press and military publications. He offered to negotiate with Micanopy, Osceola and other chiefs. But when they came to talk, Jesup took the men prisoners, holding them hostages to force the Seminoles to move under the threat of death to their leaders. Such was the situation when Taylor arrived in Florida.

Conditions seemed bad enough to Taylor that he made out a will as his first act in Florida. The Seminoles were in a murderous mood, determined to free Osceola. Taylor had been ordered to Florida not only because of his rank but also because of his skill in fighting Indians and his long experience in dealing with the Indians on a friendly and honorable basis. Taylor tried to search out chiefs with whom he could negotiate rather than fight. But his scouts were unsuccessful in finding anyone even though they waded the swamps and cut through the cypress groves. The Seminoles,

having been tricked once, were not to be deceived again by
the Americans. Arrayed against Taylor were some of the
best Seminole chiefs—Wild Cat, Sam Jones, Alligator and
the Jumper.

When peaceful attempts failed, Maj. Gen. Jesup stripped
all other military posts to assemble a 9,000-man army which
he considered "a sufficient force for every purpose, either in
the field or coming on."

Colonel Taylor was in command of operations to the south
and east of Tampa Bay, an assignment which thrust him
into the thick of the combat. He marshaled his men, baggage and rations and moved out towards the Kissimmee
River, fighting and establishing depots as he went. Taylor
sent his supplies forward under heavy guard, then brought
up his troops. Two forts, Fraser and Gardiner, had been
started when the Jumper and Oulatoochee came forward
and surrendered to Taylor. The chiefs brought about 100
Seminole fighters with them. The capitulation of these two
men seemed to augur well for Taylor's campaign, but the
optimism was chimerical. Taylor received word that all negotiations with the Indians had been broken off and that he
should now apply all possible armed exertion. That simple
order was to cost hundreds of lives and millions of dollars.

". . . Only a bloody struggle could convince the redskins
of the whites' determination to carry the campaign forward
to success," historian Holman Hamilton wrote. Taylor was
using Delaware and Shawnee Indians as scouts to probe the
Seminole lines. There were 834 other troops with Taylor
when he located the camp of Alligator, Sam Jones and Wild
Cat. Slaughtered cattle lay about, fires still smoldered and
other supplies had been left behind. Taylor's scouts captured four Seminoles, who revealed where the other Indians
had gone. The enemy was then, Taylor said, "occupying one
of the strongest and most difficult places to approach and
enter in Florida."

At noon on Christmas Day of 1837, Taylor deployed his men in extended order and moved slowly across open grass land toward a swamp, its surface spiked with saw glass. The Seminoles' position lay about a mile behind the morass. The horses of the mounted rifleman began floundering, and Taylor ordered all to dismount. It was slow slogging through the swamp, the knee-deep water making footing difficult. Taylor faced 380 well-entrenched Seminoles led by three skilled chiefs. They were sheltered by palmettoes festooned with Spanish moss. The Indians held their fire until Capt. George Allen's two companies of dismounted riflemen sloshed within range. Then the Indians each selected a human target. Alligator gave the signal, and the Indians' galling fire whittled down the ranks of the Americans. A score of the soldiers slumped down the swamp and disappeared. Colonel Gentry was mortally wounded, and the same slug which pierced him glanced and broke the arm of his son, who was acting as aide. With the loss of some officers, the untrained militiamen broke ranks and fled from the fighting.

Taylor's regulars moved quickly into the gap left by the rattled militiamen. The infantrymen quickened the charge toward the Seminoles despite the murderous fire. The Americans continued to fall. All the officers of the advance unit were either killed or wounded, but they moved relentlessly until solid ground was gained. Taylor sent a detachment around the Seminoles' flank to turn them.

As Taylor's First Infantry approached, the Seminoles fired one final volley and then slipped away toward the shore of Lake Okeechobee, their retreat gradually becoming a rout.

Taylor could claim a victory, but it was at a high cost. Twenty-eight were dead and 112 more wounded.

To relieve the agony of the wounded and to facilitate removal of the dead, Taylor had a footbridge constructed across the swamp.

"Here I experienced one of the most trying scenes of my

life," Taylor said, "and he who could have looked on with indifference, his nerves must have been differently organized from my own." Taylor watched with dismay the dead and wounded being removed to the rear. Continued pursuit was impossible because of the losses he had suffered; but Taylor immediately reorganized his men and supplies to prepare for more action. And there were numerous battles and skirmishes in which Taylor took field command, fighting beside his troops.

As he had once been brevetted for gallantry at Fort Harrison, Taylor was now brevetted as brigadier general for his distinguished services at the Battle of Lake Okeechobee. Though this promotion meant a great deal to Taylor, he was equally proud of the fact that he was popular with his men. He slept on the ground with them, ate the same food and was always ready to advance with his troops. He was as casual about battle dangers as he was about his uniforms.

To the dismay of his fellow officers, General Taylor moved about without an escort or, at best, with a minimal guard if conditions warranted it. His indifference to danger might well have been a protection, because all Indians, including Seminoles, respected personal bravery even from enemies. General Taylor was easily identified by his "Old Rough and Ready" uniform (jumper, straw hat and similar bosky items of apparel) and by his tendency to ride ahead of his troops or alone.

Hostilities continued unabated into the summer. Jesup was operating in the north and east and Col. Persifor Smith in the Coolsahatchee River. Taylor was based at Fort Bassinger, from which forays were made against the Indians. But after their major defeat by Taylor, the Indians could not be enticed into a pitched battle. His victory had been decisive in dampening the fiery spirit of the Seminoles. All that was possible now was to deny them rest, safety and comfort.

Jesup's troops continued to scour the swamps and ever-

glades, often using dogs to locate Indians. There was a great
public outcry when 33 bloodhounds were imported from
Cuba at the cost of several thousand dollars. Wild stories
were circulated about the dogs tearing Seminoles and runaway slaves to pieces. Even the President came in for public
criticism and was accused of being a heartless killer. The
fears were unfounded. The hounds, trained to follow the Negroes, somehow couldn't track the Seminoles. A few dogs
did locate the Seminoles and quickly became their pets. The
Indians trained the dogs to attack the Americans!

Shortly after that public criticism, Taylor replaced Jesup.
He continued pressure on the Seminoles, finally capturing
Alligator, along with 360 followers, during April of 1838.
There were now about 2,000 Seminoles in custody. Many
were immediately displaced to their new reservation west of
the Mississippi River.

Though Taylor was an outspoken critic of the policy to
uproot the Seminoles, he prosecuted the war diligently. He
was able to convince some Indian chiefs to surrender and
bring others with them. The capture of Alligator had been a
great psychological gain for Taylor. The Seminole squaws
were ferocious in their criticism of the chiefs who meekly
surrendered and gave up their land. Jesup had captured Osceola by trick, and the Indian leader died in prison. With
his death, the resistance weakened and the Americans continued with the final solution to the Seminole problem.

On maps, Taylor divided Florida into 20-square-mile sections and built stockades in the center of each parcel. Then
he sent troops to burn the Indian's cultivated fields, run off
their horses and destroy their villages. The Seminoles survived, being able to make bread from the coonhie root,
catch fish and kill game. Despite the hardships, they continued to launch swift, murderous attacks.

The Seminoles finally ran out of supplies and the vital energy necessary to continue the fight. When the war petered

out, the resettlement of the Seminoles began. Taylor commanded the area until April of 1839, when he was replaced by Gen. Alex Macomb. Because of his skill and experience, Taylor stayed on for another year as Indian agent. His health had suffered with the recurrent attacks of fever but life wasn't too unpleasant, because there were three members of his family with him: his brother, Capt. Joe Taylor, fought with the General at Lake Okeechobee; Dr. Robert Wood was staff physician for his father-in-law; and Mrs. Taylor had joined the General at Fort Brooke.

Finally on May 6, 1840, Taylor was relieved of assignment in the Florida theater of operations. He turned his command over to Gen. Walker Armistead. There was high praise for Taylor from Joel R. Poinsett, Secretary of War, who said the Florida campaign had been "conducted with vigor and ability under that zealous and indefatigable officer Brig. Gen. Taylor, who accomplished all that could be expected with the very limited means at his command. . . ."

The war against the Seminoles continued until 1843, and sporadically thereafter to 1857. And with General Taylor's relief from duty with the Army of the South, he commented: "My days of ambition are passed. . . ."

Six

MARKING TIME

General and Mrs. Taylor were able to visit relatives and old friends during the six-month furlough which had been granted Taylor following his duty in Florida. His health had suffered noticeably during the Second Seminole War, and he needed time to rest and recuperate.

Following a debriefing session in Washington, Taylor was ordered to Baton Rouge, an assignment which delighted both Taylors. His wife chose a delapidated river-view cottage for their home, rather than using the more substantial officer's quarters to which Taylor was entitled. She quickly converted it into a quaint, rose-covered home. It became the center for both social and church affairs. Mrs. Taylor was a devout Episcopalian and started a chapel to provide religious services. General Taylor was indifferent about formal religion, though he was Christian and generous in donations to churches and charities.

Shortly after arriving there, Taylor bought a large cotton plantation, Cypress Grove, near the site of Rodney, Mississippi. It proved costly because of flooding, but Taylor stubbornly operated the place.

The idylls of home life were interrupted when General Taylor took command of the Second Military Department, with headquarters at Fort Gibson, near the confluence of the

Arkansas and Neosho rivers. Taylor was able to take his family to Fort Smith, about 60 miles from his headquarters.

Both forts outraged Taylor's sense of careful money husbandry and management. Construction and repair expenses were exorbitant, and such things as 15-foot stone walls, massive blockhouses and bastions would "serve as a lasting monument of the folly of those who planned, as well as him who had the same executed." Because Taylor estimated that costs would outweigh actual value, work was stopped on Fort Gibson. But residents there protested that the fort be maintained, not only for protection but as an economic factor along the frontier. They prevailed with the Congressman, and Taylor was kept exceedingly busy with the military, civilian and Indian affairs.

The Chickasaws, Kickapoos, Shawnees and Caddoes couldn't get along with each other, and the Texans who frequently stole across the Red River to harass the Indians or steal their stock didn't get along with any of the tribes. To maintain peace, Taylor ordered construction of Fort Washita at the junction of the Red and Washita rivers. It was the most westerly point of contact with the Indians, and would accommodate the traders, trappers and hunters of the area.

Withal, Taylor was also trying to keep up with the noisiest presidential campaign to occur in a long time, which involved some of his friends. William Henry Harrison and John Tyler were running against President Martin Van Buren and Richard Johnson. It was a bitter campaign, with General Harrison picturing Van Buren as an aristocrat who wore corsets and perfumed his beard with cologne. Opponents described Harrison as a country bumpkin who lived in a log cabin and existed on hard cider. It was during this campaign that the enduring political phrase "Tippecanoe and Tyler too" was coined. It was a reference to Harrison's battle with the Indian chief called the Prophet.

Though the odds favored Van Buren, Harrison romped in

with 234 electoral votes to Van Buren's 60. But victory was short-lived, because President Harrison lived only 32 days in office and was succeeded by Tyler on April 6, 1841. Harrison was the first President to die in office.

Tyler had a working majority in the House, but there was an edge against him in the Senate. He managed to push through a high tariff bill and vetoed all efforts to establish a national bank. Because of Tyler's policies, all but one member of his Cabinet resigned.

Tyler, a Virginian, was vociferously in favor of annexing Texas, as were many Southerners. But Tyler favored obtaining Texas as a state through peaceful negotiation and treaties. Because of the violent objections from the Mexicans and the reluctance of Congress to do anything at all, the matter remained unresolved.

Taylor was genuinely saddened by the death of his old friend Harrison. Uncertain about the qualities of Tyler, Taylor exercised discretion and said nothing publicly about his opinions. He had many duties of his own to complete.

One was attendance at the various Indian councils convened within his jurisdiction. A most significant conference was held on May 2, 1842, at Deep Fork, not far from Fort Gibson. More than 2,000 Indians, representing 16 tribes, attended. The Deep Fork meeting was called to redress grievances between tribes and enhance the prestige of the Creek Nation. General Taylor seized it as an opportunity to express his own feelings, and to explain the policy of his government. Taylor cautioned the Indians to be extremely careful not to cause any incident during the times of sensitive relations between Texas and Mexico. The Indians agreed, though most of them were more interested in parochial affairs.

The Osages mistakenly believed the meeting was called to exchange stolen stock, but when none of the other tribes brought anything to trade for the stolen horses, the Osages stole 30 head of stock from the Kiowas and rode off. Taylor skillfully mediated the incident, and there was no bloodshed.

The Indians all wore their most colorful costumes; their faces were painted, and their heads were decorated with feathers or festoons of bright cloth. Taylor and his aides looked drab by comparison as they bade farewell. "All seemed animated with a desire to cultivate peaceable relations with our government and with each other," Taylor reported afterwards.

Taylor displayed his consummate skill in dealing with the Indians when a month-long council was convened during the following year. This was larger than the first meeting. Treaties were drawn to establish the independence and autonomy of the various Indian nations. Another document was drawn to suppress the whiskey trade. The Cherokees were so impressed with Taylor's sympathetic understanding of the Indians' problems that they laid out a town on the site of the council grounds, named Tahlequah (Oklahoma), and built a brick courthouse and a brick house for Taylor and his family because they wanted him to live there among the Cherokees.

". . . Taylor's simplicity and directness had won the confidence of most of the Indians," Silas McKinley wrote. "He had the confidence of even the Seminoles, whom he defeated at Okeechobee when they were transferred to districts which he supervised. . . ."

General Taylor was desolate when he witnessed the plight of the Seminoles, who now lived in the most abject poverty. Many of them were ill, all of them emaciated. They had never been able to adjust to either the climate or the conditions of the resettlement area and had deteriorated into little more than animals. Once more the United States had failed to honor its treaty agreements with America's first residents.

When Harrison had been elected President, Taylor urged his friend to provide both a better military organization and understanding treatment of the Indians. But Harrison's untimely death prevented any consideration of the proposals, and President Tyler ignored the suggestions. Later, a portion of Taylor's plan for a more effcient army organization was adopted. Then, abruptly as he had come, Taylor was ordered to the New Orleans area in 1843, and he moved his family to Baton Rouge.

Taylor's area command was reduced when he changed to the New Orleans area, but it was a more important position. His headquarters were at Fort Jesup, the American fort nearest the occupied portion of Texas.

A sidelight on Taylor's softening attitude to a life in the army came about when he assigned Capt. William Wallace Bliss as a staff aide. The young man, usually called "Perfect" Bliss, was in love with Taylor's daughter Betty. The General approved of the match between them even though she would be the third daughter to marry an army officer. Taylor liked Bliss personally and respected his intelligence and wit. Unlike the stubborn resistance he offered when Lieut. Jeff Davis wanted to marry Knox, Taylor now "expressed no misgivings about having another army man in the family." The young couple were not able to marry for several years, because of Bliss's military assignments, but eventually they were wed. Bliss remained as Taylor's aide and assisted, at least in part, with some of the memorable military dispatches which were later issued over General Taylor's signature.

Ostensibly, General Taylor's duties at Fort Jesup were to keep the border Indians and Texans from each others' throats and away from each others' horses. Five companies of Dragoons, or mounted riflemen, were assigned to Taylor's command to control the situation. There were several border incidents involving the troops, the Texans and the Mexicans, which enraged all of the people and made the situation even more delicate.

But the Texans were becoming embroiled in a larger issue, which was rapidly approaching a violent conclusion.

From the moment President Tyler assumed office, he had advocated the peaceful annexation of Texas, and when Abel Upshur became Secretary of State, negotiations were finally undertaken. Texas President Sam Houston, realizing the vengeance which lurked in the Mexicans' hearts, insisted that the United States provide military protection for the Texans while the talks continued. Houston requested that ample soldiers be assigned to the area and that naval vessels be stationed in the Gulf of Mexico to be in position if hostilities began. William Murphy, consul to Texas, assured the Texans that protection would be provided, but Washington rescinded the agreement.

President Tyler said that military protection could only be provided after a formal treaty was signed and when Texas had become the responsibility of the United States. With this pressure applied, a treaty was signed on April 12, 1844. American warships were concentrated in the Gulf, and General Taylor's command at Fort Jesup was now dubbed "a corps of observation . . . in readiness for service at any moment." Taylor was given the option of moving into the Sabine River area if he believed the situation demanded it. But he was officially warned against moving farther without additional instructions and permission.

Whatever previous feeling Taylor might have entertained about the army and Washington officials, he realized that being given command of this sensitive key post was a mark of high confidence in his judgment and discretion to act only with patience and prudence in a crisis if it should arise. Taylor had no reservations about his ability to meet and resolve any situation.

Following receipt of his orders, Taylor dispatched Capt.

L. J. Beall of the Second Dragoons to inform President Houston that there were 1,000 men alerted for any emergency. Beall was also instructed to make a full reconnaissance of the terrain during the trip. Taylor seldom missed an opportunity to fully exploit a situation for his best advantage. Beall's errand could do double duty, for Taylor believed a move into Texas would eventually be made, and all available military intelligence should be gathered.

Other than routine garrison duty, there was little for Taylor and his men to do except watch and wait. Taylor studied the gathering political storm which preceded the 1844 Presidential elections. Henry Clay, a long-time friend of Taylor's, was running for the office, and his philosophy paralleled the views held by Taylor. Both men believed that the forcible annexation of Texas would result in war with Mexico. Accordingly, both men opposed it. (The Whigs and Abolitionists in the Senate joined forces to defeat confirmation of the treaty which had already been negotiated, and the Texas question remained unresolved.) President Tyler sought reelection, but he had destroyed his Whig support because of opposition to the establishment of a national banking system comparable with the English arrangement. Tyler, lacking the support of his own party, was not strong enough politically to establish a splinter party which could successfully sponsor him as a candidate.

Henry Clay, 67, was nominated on the first ballot when the Whig Party held their presidential convention in the Universalist Church of Baltimore, Maryland, on May 1, 1844. Theodore Frelinghuysen of New Jersey was named as vice-presidential candidate.

Near the end of May, the Democratic Party held its nominating convention at the Odd Fellows Hall in Baltimore. James Knox Polk, a lawyer by education but a politician in philosophy, even though he had never aspired to high office, had spent many years in Congress and had been Speaker of the House several times. Voting at the convention became deadlocked for the first seven ballots between President Van Buren and Lewis Cass of Michigan. Polk's name was offered on the next ballot, and he was nominated unanimously as a compromise candidate on the ninth ballot. Silas Wright was suggested as his running mate, but he declined. George M. Dallas was then chosen.

Despite Polk's long public record, the Whigs tried to deride and minimize his importance by asking, "Who is James K. Polk?" The Whigs learned to their sorrow that Polk was an astute politician. Clay may have helped Polk's election as much as any other one person. Clay tried to avoid discussion of the Texas situation, even though it was a smoldering, vital issue. Polk trumpeted the policy of "Manifest Destiny," which urged the expansion of the United States. Polk was vocal about the independence of Texas and the need to have California made a part of the United States. That was rough language which pioneers understood and the kind of talk the rest of America wanted to hear.

Polk was an unprepossessing-looking man, slight, spare, with a small head, gray eyes and long, graying hair. He was shy, but a determined, narrow partisan of the Democratic Party. Polk's mild appearance might have beguiled Clay into saying that he could defeat Polk "with my left hand." Polk spoke solemnly of acquiring Texas and California, and the fighting slogan of "Fifty-Four Forty or Fight" indicated that Polk meant to have Oregon as well. Clay, even if he had wanted, couldn't have matched those grandiose plans.

Clay stood frozen as he was handed a slip of paper while he was attending a "victory" election party. Polk had beaten him by 38,000 votes. Clay recovered quickly, poured another glass of sherry and, raising the glass, said: "I drink to the health and happiness of everyone here."

Clay then announced his defeat. His apparent unconcern with the election was a facade. After others left, Clay remarked: "The late blow that has fallen on our country is heavy. I hope that she may recover from it, but I confess that the prospect ahead is dark and discouraging."

There were sound reasons for Clay's misgivings, especially after "lame duck" President Tyler was rebuffed trying to push through the rejected treaty for the annexation of Texas. Sam Houston was equally sensitive about the Congressional attitude. Making his farewell address after serving two terms as president of Texas, Houston said: "The attitude of Texas is now one of peculiar interest. The United States has spurned her. Let her, therefore, work out her own political salvation."

Hotheads in Texas immediately demanded that Texas claim California, and there were thinly veiled hints about secession by the southern and southwestern states to form a new nation because the United States was declining in strength and influence. "A rival power will be built up," a Texan said, adding that Texas would be that rival.

President Tyler agreed in part, then shaped a situation which made it incumbent upon Polk to annex Texas, no matter what his own political opinions. Tyler managed to get a joint Congressional resolution approved which said that Texas would enter the Union as a state—not as a territory, which was the usual method. Tyler was able to get it passed, since it required only a simple majority to pass instead of the two-thirds needed for a formal treaty. The gambit was wonderfully clever politics.

When President Tyler left the White House, his second wife, Julia Gardiner Tyler, wore a black dress and bonnet and around her neck hung the "immortal gold pen"—the one with which her husband had signed the enabling resolution to admit Texas.

The beginning of Polk's term was bleak and dreary, with rain pouring down on the day of inauguration Tuesday, March 4, 1845. Despite the bad weather, Tyler and Polk

rode to the ceremonies in an open carriage, both men bow-
ing to the throngs which lined the route.

With the formalities over, Polk plunged into the affairs of
state handcuffed to a policy of admitting Texas to the Union.
He was also committed to his policy of "Manifest Destiny,"
a catch phrase coined by John L. O'Sullivan, a reporter for
the *Democratic Review*. Polk liked the term. To him it was a
synonym for unrealized American dreams of peaceful expansion, even though to some it was an ominous slogan which
called up visions of unrelenting aggression. "This country
had elevated to power an administration pledged to an im-
perialist program," historian McKinley wrote.

There was ample precedent for it from the time fearless
Yankee merchantmen sailed their Boston ships to the tran-
quil bay of Monterey on the California coast and traded
some bolts of cotton for pelts and cowhides. Mountain men
Ewing Young and James Ohio Pattie had been pushing to
the far west. John C. Frémont had made some scientific expeditions with federal sanction and later helped establish an
independent state within California, the Bear Flag Republic.
Moses Austin and his son Stephen made a contract to bring
300 families into the Texas area. Once the Yankees had their
noses under the Mexican national tent, they never withdrew.

President Polk brought men into his Cabinet with similar
views regarding the expansion of the United States.

The gathering storm, the rehearsal for conflict was increasingly apparent, and Gen. Taylor was not at all surprised
when he received secret orders to move from Fort Jesup "to
the mouth of the Sabine River, or to such other point in the
Gulf of Mexico, or its navigable waters, as in your judgment
may be the most convenient for an embarkation at the
proper time for the western frontier of Texas." Secretary of
State James Buchanan's orders to Taylor were dated June
15, 1845, and Taylor received them two weeks later.

Taylor got things in motion immediately. By July 3, the

Fourth Infantry was on its way from Fort Jesup to New Orleans. It was followed shortly by the Third Infantry. Dragoons saddled their horses, and teamsters prepared wagons and animals for the long march, which for some would end in Mexico City, for others in death. On July 9, General Taylor kissed his wife and daughter Betty good-bye, then rode off.

General Taylor had turned 60 years of age while the debate over Texas raged. He had grown rather paunchy, waiting his time to be a hero. Over the years his face had acquired the bronze of the sun, his keen eyes peered out from a quiver of crow's feet at the corners, and his face was shaped, beneath his straw hat, with long gray hair and sideburns. Often there was the suggestion of a smile twitching at the corners of his wide mouth. In all he looked the part of a rural resident, a farmer, rather than a courageous general on his way to fight and win a successive string of battles for his country.

Taylor received supplementary orders from Andrew J. Donelson, charge d'affaires, in Texas. He was instructed not to make any move into Texas until he was formally notified that the annexation of Texas had been accomplished or received other orders to mount an attack.

En route to New Orleans, Taylor heard that Texas had been admitted but the resolution had to be confirmed at a constitutional convention scheduled for July 4. Agreement seemed assured.

With that, Taylor planned to assemble his troops at New Orleans first, then move on to Corpus Christi, situated at the mouth of the Nueces River. Taylor chose the site because of supply problems by sea. It was also described as being "healthy as Pensacola," an estimate which would soon be open to dispute.

General Taylor's Army of Observation had now become an Army of Occupation.

Seven

INVESTMENT OF TROOPS

The streets of New Orleans throbbed with activity as Taylor's Army of Occupation prepared to board their vessels and invade Mexican territory.

". . . The moon was just rising as we marched out, gilding the domes and the house-tops and caused our bayonets to glisten in the mellow light. The deep shadows on one side of the street, the bright moonlight on the other, the solemn quiet of the sleeping city disturbed so harshly by the martial music of the column," Capt. William S. Henry, a recent West Point graduate, wrote poetically of their leave taking from New Orleans on July 25, 1845.

General Taylor was aboard the Alabama with his staff officers, including Captain Bliss, his aide, and elements of the Third, Fourth and Seventh Infantry, Capt. Braxton Bragg's artillery, 20 Dragoons, quartermasters and other essentials for a long campaign. There were men aboard who would later become illustrious figures in military annals—U. S. Grant, George Gordon Meade, Jeff Davis, Albert S. Johnston and many others who were now honing their military skills for greater careers.

Several sailing vessels heavily laden with men and supplies followed the Alabama as she slipped her moorings at 3 A.M. The convoy was escorted by the sloop of war St. Marys.

74

The course was set for Corpus Christi, located inside Arkansas Bay on the west bank of the Nueces, but the real course was one set for war with Mexico. To Taylor's mind, the adventure might prove to be unnecessarily hazardous because he fully expected Mexican troops numbering 7,000 or 8,000 strong.

In contrast, the entire authorized strength of the United States army in 1845 was 8,613, which included the general staff officers. Even so, the actual strength of the army was about 7,200 men, and they were scattered over more than 200 military posts throughout the United States. Taylor shrugged as he considered the relative figures. Taylor would fight the best he could with what he had. That was all anyone was expected to do. Taylor was determined to make the best possible use of the 1,500 men under his command.

After sailing for two days without incident, Taylor's invasion force landed safely on St. Joseph's Island, despite high winds and rough seas. Morale improved greatly when the men breakfasted on fresh fish and oysters.

Next day, Taylor led his men in shallow draught boats across the narrow strip of water to the banks of the Nueces River, where he ordered that a camp be established. Because of the shallow water and the rough weather, several boats were upset, with their supplies lost or waterlogged. One steamer blew up and killed several men. But the landing was accomplished, the troops invested. Taylor would remain there for the next seven months awaiting the outcome of diplomatic maneuvers in Washington and Mexico City. By September, Taylor's command swelled to about 4,000 men, more than half of the entire authorized American army. Taylor's encampment stretched for more than a mile along the beach and at least 500 yards back from the shoreline.

Corpus Christi was a small village of probably less than 100 residents when Taylor arrived. It was ruled by a Texas "colonel" named Henry L. Kinney, whose sole interest was converting anything he could into the Yankee dollar. It didn't make any difference what it was—horses, mules, women, Indians or weapons. Kinney warmly welcomed Taylor and his tiny army, and provided Taylor with accurate intelligence reports about the Mexican troop movements. Taylor could safely ignore reports from Washington that the Mexicans might attack at any time.

For a time, living near the village was pleasant for the troops. They could swim, hunt and fish, and even luxuriate in the sun mellowed by gentle sea breezes. Besides, there were other earthly delights available in Corpus Christi, whose population had exploded following the occupation by Taylor's troops. Gamblers, lawyers, saloon keepers, prostitutes, hair dressers and photographers trooped into the village. A newspaper was started and a theater opened. It was an atmosphere conducive to gambling, stealing, drinking, brawling and other disorders following the use of the rot-gut whiskey.

"Almost all of the houses in Corpus Christi are drinking houses put up since our arrival," one of Taylor's officers wrote home.

Taylor didn't exercise any military authority in village activities, even though he neither indulged in nor approved of the misconduct which occurred there. Taylor had confidence that his men would be ready to fight when they were needed, and that was his principal concern. Besides the troops were kept busy foraging for firewood, mending their clothes and their tents and making surveys in adjacent areas, principally between the Nueces and Rio Grande rivers or as far as was safe. Other men broke and trained horses which were readily available for about three dollars a head.

Subordinate officers sniped, in letters, at Taylor's failure to sternly discipline the fractious soldiers. It was difficult for some to reconcile Taylor's previous antipathy to alcohol and gambling. One officer went so far as to write that he "didn't have the slightest confidence" in Taylor's abilities as a field commander. "If Taylor succeeds, it will be by accident," another remarked. But Lieut. George Meade, an excellent officer who would later lead divisions at Antietam and Fredericksburg and defeat Lee at Gettysburg, said: "Gen. Taylor has his own views and plans and does not trouble himself with those of other people."

Criticism mounted, however, as the balmy weather gave way to winter storms, carrying with them incessant rain and cold and cutting winds. Army tents proved to be faulty, thin and leaky, providing scant protection from the driving rains. Men went for days without dry clothes or beds, since there was also a scarcity of dry fuel. What wood was available fired the cook stoves. Sanitation and camp policing was slack, and the men began to fall ill with diarrhea, dysentery, fevers and assorted debilities until more than 10 per cent of the entire command was on the sick list. Rattlesnakes, chiggers and bed bugs infested the camp; lightning killed two soldiers, and morale ebbed away.

There was nothing much Taylor could do to relieve the illness or the intrigues, because he was awaiting orders from Washington. So long as he wasn't being attacked or even threatened, Taylor could only wait.

President Polk, his course to acquire Texas unchanged, was still trying to negotiate peacefully with the Mexican government. In November of 1845, Senator John Sliddel of Louisiana was sent as minister plenipotentiary and envoy extraordinary and armed with authority to settle American claims, and to discuss other matters with the Mexican officials. Sliddel was also instructed to settle the final Texas boundary along the course of the Rio Grande.

Mexico had been in a constant state of turmoil, and the

government was so unstable that it was almost impossible to establish diplomatic relations with a Mexican president before he was deposed.

When Sliddel left for his mission to Mexico, José Joaquin de Herrera was president. He had been elected in the previous September. In those two months, Herrera had come under political attack by opponents who insisted that Sliddel be rebuffed, a move which would affront the hated Yankees. If Sliddel was received, the diplomatic recognition would imply the existence of friendly relations between Mexico and the United States, and suggest that the Texas question would be settled on American terms. That would never do, some Mexicans said. As a result, Sliddel waited in the outer offices of the ambassador, getting no answer to his inquiries. Disgustedly, Sliddel informed Washington of his official insult. He then withdrew to Jalapa to await developments. In the meantime, Texas was formally admitted into the United States on December 29, 1845.

Herrera was overthrown by Gen. Mariano Parades, who assumed office in January, 1846. President Polk believed that all hope of compromise vanished with Parades in charge. Sliddel's report reached Washington January 12, 1846, and confirmed the official opinion that Parades would insist upon a settlement along the Sabine River, which separated Texas from Louisiana.

The next day, Secretary of War William L. Marcy, issued orders to Taylor.

". . . Advance and occupy, with the troops under your command, positions on or near the east bank of the Rio del Norte [Rio Grande] as soon as it can be conveniently done with reference to the season and the routes by which your movements must be made. . . ."

But he softened the order by adding: "It is not designed in our present relations with Mexico, that you should treat her as an enemy; but, should she assume that character, by a declaration of war, or any open act of hostility toward us, you will not act merely on the defensive, if your relative means enable you to do otherwise. . . ."

The United States naval forces were alerted to the changing, menacing conditions. Commodore David Conners, whose flotilla had been withdrawn from Mexican waters while Sliddel was trying to negotiate peacefully, was ordered to return to the Mexican coast and, if war came, seize both Tampico and Vera Cruz. Commodore John D. Sloat, in command of the Pacific squadron, was issued orders to seize California ports under the necessary circumstances. Since the Mexicans had publicly proclaimed that the occupation of any portions of Texas by American troops would be considered an act of war, Taylor was completely aware of what might ensue when he left Corpus Christi.

Because there was no urgency stressed in Marcy's orders to advance, Taylor waited until the weather was amenable and his men improved in health. It was five weeks later, March 8, 1846, before Taylor believed it was appropriate to move out. Spring had now pulled away the shroud of winter.

During the interim, Taylor sent out reconnaissance parties to inspect the line of march which they would follow. Lieutenant Grant reported that the route included not a single habitation, cultivated field or herd of domestic animals.

An advance column of Dragoons, moving ahead of Maj. Sam Ringgold's "flying artillery," led Taylor's troops. Three days later, General Taylor, with his headquarters staff left Corpus Christi, much to the dismay of the residents there who had circulated rumors of all sorts to delay or stop the departure of the rich Americans. Even though most of the supplies were sent ahead to Port Isabel by ship under the care of Major John Munroe, there were still 307 heavily laden wagons moving with Taylor's troops. About 75 were pulled by oxen, and the rest by mules or draft horses.

"The roads are in good order," Taylor reported, "the
weather fine and the troops in excellent condition for service." It was good that they started out in prime condition because four days after leaving Corpus Christi on the 196-mile
march, they encountered a 65-mile strip of sandy wasteland,
almost completely barren of vegetation. But they resolutely
continued the advance. Taylor, like the others, suffered from
sunburned, wind-lashed face and hands and a lack of water
and fresh supplies. Some of the men suffered dreadfully
from thirst, but Taylor gave no sign of discomfort even
though he limited himself to no more than the least of his
men.

"Very hot . . . great scarcity of water . . . men suffer
greatly," Dr. Madison Mills, regimental surgeon, told his
diary during the march. "Some of the men had fallen, others
could scarcely keep up. . . ."

After four days of privation, they overcame the desert and
found both sweet water and some wild cattle, which were
slaughtered to provide fresh meat for all of the troops.

Tight security watches were kept at night now that Taylor had advanced into an area where they might be attacked
at any time. Scouts were sent out on both flanks and the
point of the advance to counter any surprise attack. No sign
of the Mexicans was seen until March 19, when the Americans approached the Arroyo Colorado, a salt lagoon about
100 yards wide and four feet deep in some places. Across
the water, Taylor could see Mexican cavalrymen, though he
couldn't estimate their strength because of the heavy
growth of cactus and chaparral. Mexican buglers rode in
and out of the cover, blowing furiously to give the impression of a large force of men. A truce-bearing messenger
brought a dispatch from Gen. Francisco Mejía which
warned Taylor that any move across the lagoon would not
only be fatal to Taylor but an overt act of war as well.

"We will cross immediately," Taylor replied, "and if a single man of you shows his face after my men enter the water, I will open artillery fire on him."

Taylor ordered the lagoon's banks to be cut down to accommodate the heavy wagons, and all preparations were made for a crossing on the next day. Troops were brought up in a forced march, and some of the baggage wagons were left behind under guard. During the night Major Ringgold's guns and those of Captain Bragg were unlimbered to rake the Mexicans if resistance was encountered during the crossing. The cannoneers stood by their guns with matches when General Worth, his ruddy face lighted with the excitement of battle, led the assault troops across the lagoon. The four companies of "red-legged infantry" (artillerymen retrained as foot soldiers) splashed, waded and yelled, holding their muskets high as they followed Worth directly for the Mexican camp. Taylor watched tensely as the men reached the far shore and clambered up the bank. It was a time when they were almost defenseless. But there wasn't a shot fired, and Worth's men signaled that the Mexicans had fled.

With Taylor in the lead, the supply wagons rumbled on towards the Rio Grande. Taylor left the column under the command of General Worth while he veered off to Port Isabel for a rendezvous with Commodore Conners, who was to bring supplies. Where they parted, the troops were 18 miles from Matamoros, the Mexican city which stood across the Rio Grande and which would be their first point of attack.

Approaching Port Isabel, Taylor saw that the few buildings there had been set afire by fleeing Mexicans. But the flames were doused before any extensive damage was done, and the area was quickly secured. Just as that was done, Conners appeared over the horizon, and unloading operations began just as soon as the lighters could reach the ships. Once this was completed, Taylor returned to assume com-

mand of his army, and about noon of March 28, he raised
his hand to signal a halt. They had reached the east bank of
the Rio Grande at a point opposite Matamoros.

Through his glasses, General Taylor could see an immense
cathedral and rows of sturdy houses whose roofs and windows were crammed with curious Mexicans watching the
movements of the Americans. The Mexican flag flew over
Mejía's headquarters, and there were numerous Mexican soldiers in evidence.

General Taylor, his officers and enlisted men all stood at
attention and saluted when the Stars and Stripes was hauled
to the tip of a temporary flagstaff. The regimental band
played "The Star-Spangled Banner," followed by the field
music of "Yankee Doodle" with fifes and drums. A pet
rooster, which one of the soldiers had brought with him,
flapped its wings and crowed defiantly.

Taylor ordered four huge seige guns, 18-pounders, hauled
into place where they could bombard Matamoros; then he
sent Worth across the Rio Grande to assure General Mejía
that the soldiers were merely taking possession of what they
believed to be American soil and meant no mischief to Mexican interests. Mejía declared the presence of the American
troops an act of war. With the statements exchanged, Taylor
began construction of a fort which would accommodate 400
soldiers. It was called Fort Texas.

The Mexicans replied in kind and began strengthening
their fortifications. A priest publicly blessed each emplacement, sprinkling it with consecrated liquids.

It was shrewd cold war psychology. The presence of the
priest reminded many of the American soldiers of their own
religious affiliations and that Mexico was a Catholic nation.
It was a sensitive point. In the early 1840s, as increasing
numbers of European immigrants concentrated in the large
industrial cities of the United States, a splinter political

party from the Whigs, officially called the Native American Party, was formed to combat this so-called foreign threat. Since the members often met in secrecy and used terrorism to prevent immigrants from gaining citizenship and holding office, they were given the nickname "Know-Nothings," from their proverbial answer to any questions about their activities. Since the majority of the immigrants were of the Roman Catholic faith, the "Know-Nothings" also became an anti-Catholic Party. Some of the Catholic soldiers had suffered from this discrimination back in the States.

The Mexicans played on these resentments by scattering pamphlets among the Americans, and subtly reminding them of their religion through the use of the priests. The Mexicans offered 320 acres of land to all deserters, and at least 43 of the "northern barbarians," as the Yankees were described by the *Matamoros Gazette*, responded to the blandishments and swam the Rio Grande. Others were shot by American sentries as they tried to desert. From the men who made it to Matamoros, the Mexicans formed the Voluntarios Irlandesas, (Irish Volunteers), which was also called the Red Battalion because of the red hair and ruddy complexions of many of its men. The worst of the lot was John Riley of the Fifth Infantry, who was an expert artilleryman and a deserter from the Canadian army. "Juan Reyley," as the Mexicans called him, was a leader in the infamous San Patricio Battalion which caused Taylor great difficulty at the battle of Buena Vista.

"We have such a superiority in artillery that it is impossible for them with any force to drive us from here," Lieutenant Meade wrote. Other officers were not as optimistic, and work progressed steadily. At the same time, the Mexicans began harassing guerrilla activity. One raid resulted in the death of Col. Trueman Cross, Taylor's quartermaster officer, who had ridden out of bounds and was shot down by the Mexicans and his body hidden. His death was not discovered for ten days, and not before a search party officer, 2nd Lieut. Theodore Porter, was also slain.

In the meantime, Gen. Pedro de Ampudia assumed command at Matamoros. He was a brave, skilled and cruel officer who had once boiled in oil the head of a political opponent. With him were 3,000 troops. Ampudia sent word to Taylor that he must leave the area within 24 hours or suffer extreme consequences.

General Taylor calmly ignored the demand and intensified work on Fort Texas. He asked Commodore Conners to blockade the mouth of the Rio Grande with his vessels, which would keep the Mexicans from getting any supplies by water. About then Cross's mangled body, with his skull crushed, was found.

"Hostilities may be considered as commenced," General Taylor informed Washington, though it was weeks before the news actually reached President Polk.

Mexican General Ampudia was still shaking his head and muttering about Taylor's incredible military impudence when he was replaced by Gen. Mariano Arista, a stately Mexican who had once lived in Cincinnati. Arista carried orders from Presidente Parades to begin military operations against the Americans immediately upon his arrival at Matamoros. Arista's arrival was greeted with great pomp and ceremony, but with that over, Arista got down to the business of fighting a war.

Gen. Anastasio Torrejon was sent across the Rio Grande in command of a large cavalry force. Their blue uniforms, trousers with red piping and red pennants made a colorful display of martial strength as they searched through the chaparral looking for vagrant American patrols.

A friendly native told Taylor of Torrejon's activities, and he ordered Capt. Seth Thornton with 63 men to investigate and report on their movements. Thornton's slight, almost frail appearance belied his wildly brave demeanor. But he was beguiled into a hopeless trap by a treacherous guide and was surrounded by 1,600 of Torrejon's men. Sixteen of the American Dragoons were killed immediately, and the rest were clubbed to the ground as they tried to escape. Many of the men were wounded, and all survivors were taken prisoner. Thornton was later exchanged for Mexican prisoners, though he had been reported dead in initial reports of the ambush.

Intelligence reports indicated that Port Isabel was being attacked. Another outpost had been assaulted, leaving five dead and four wounded. This was war, and there was no doubt about that. Taylor realized that the situation was perilous. With fewer than 3,000 men, Taylor faced 6,000 or 8,-000 Mexicans! Hurriedly he sent dispatches off to Washington and requests to the governors of Texas and Louisiana asking for reinforcements. He asked for 5,000 three-month vounteers, which would bridge the gap until Congress could amend the laws and provide regular troops for the army.

Old Rough and Ready acted quickly and decisively to meet the critical situation. Under the command of Maj. Jacob Brown, Taylor left the Seventh Infantry, Bragg's artillery and about 500 other men at Fort Texas. Then, at 4 A.M. on May 1, he set out for Port Isabel. There Taylor hoped to obtain weapons, ammunition and other supplies before the Mexicans moved in behind him and cut off the supply route to the sea and Connors' ships.

Taylor's move was astute. Arista had planned to straddle the road between Port Isabel and Fort Texas, but a temporary shortage of boats delayed his crossing of the Rio Grande. By the time Arista's troops had reached the eastern shore, Taylor had ridden past on his way to Port Isabel.

Once again there was astounding timing between Taylor and Conners. Five hundred marines were being landed to reinforce Taylor's tiny army. Useful supplies were quickly stowed into the wagons, and on the morning of May 3 the ominous thunder of distant guns was in the air. Taylor realized that the Mexicans were attacking Fort Texas, only 12 miles away. He assigned Capt. Sam Walker and four other Texas Rangers to investigate. By the next dawn, Walker was able to wriggle through the enemy picket lines into Fort Texas to talk with Major Brown.

Brown said that the American artillery, the large seige guns, had silenced most of the Mexican weapons during the opening barrages just as Lieutenant Meade estimated. Mortar shells were still being lobbed into the fort, but the Americans had built sandbag shelters which were reinforced with timbers and earth-filled barrels. Casualties had been very light even among the unprotected animals. Brown's only real concern was the growing shortage of ammunition to continue the artillery exchange. Walker reported the cheerful news to Taylor, and work was speeded for the return trip.

It was midafternoon of May 7 before Taylor was ready to move. By then, scouts reported that Mexican troops were deployed across the road which led to Fort Texas. A battle was shaping up. Taylor had 2,200 men to face an estimated 6,000 Mexican troops.

". . . The General has every confidence in his officers and men," Taylor wrote in his formal orders for the day. ". . . He has no doubt of the result, let the enemy meet him in what numbers they may. He wishes to enjoin upon the battalions of infantry that their main dependence must be in the bayonet. . . ."

Morale was generally high, though some green troops were jittery. Most were quieted with the assurances from seasoned officers, who told them that scarcely one shot in a thousand found its human target during any battle. Those odds seemed to satisfy the men.

Leaving late in the day, Taylor's column traveled little

more than five miles the first day. Resuming the march at daylight, the scouts reported Mexican troops ahead near the ponds at Palo Alto ("tall tree"), about a mile ahead. There were Mexican cavalry units on both flanks, with infantry supported by cannon in the center, all athwart the road to Fort Texas. Scouts estimated that there were 6,000 men, and they had seen General Arista taking active command.

Taylor rode up on his favorite mount, "Old Whitey," using his glasses to survey the situation. He slouched, one leg slung over the pommel of his saddle, chewing tobacco and looking for all the world like a farmer deciding what section to plow rather than a general planning battle strategy. He peered through his glasses from time to time, then looking away to consider what he had seen. In time, he ordered his men to stack their arms, a section at a time, fill their canteens and rest as best they could before the oncoming fight. It was hot and dusty, and the men had already marched 12 miles that day. With his wagons parked and Captain May's Second Dragoons on guard, the two 18-pound cannons, drawn by oxen, moved a short distance up the road. The Third Infantry, supported by Ringgold's artillery, was on the right flank; the Fourth Infantry was on the left, with Capt. Jim Duncan's artillery in support; the Fifth and Eighth Infantry regiments formed the right and left flanks.

Sword in hand, Taylor signaled the advance. The battle of Palo Alto began on May 8, 1846. It was the first time that American troops had fought another civilized nation since the battle of New Orleans.

Eight

THE BATTLE OF
PALO ALTO

"If the enemy oppose my march, in whatever force, I shall fight him," Taylor said before the battle. He was making the statement a reality as his troops opened the attack on the Mexican forces arrayed at Palo Alto.

Submitting to the logic of his artillery officers—Ringgold, Duncan and Bragg—General Taylor decided to use cannon rather than close-quarter combat against the Mexicans. The muskets and rifles used by the American troops were not much better than those possessed by the Mexicans. Besides, the Mexican numbers were superior. But the American cannon were much better, and the marksmanship of the American batteries was excellent. As soon as the Mexicans began firing, Taylor withdrew his foot troops and thrust the artillery into the forefront. Ringgold and Duncan responded eagerly to the task.

"*Viva la Republica*," General Arista shouted, and his horse danced with excitement. The Mexican General's strategy had been a massed infantry attack against the Americans. He believed his troops could overwhelm the smaller army led by Taylor. But Arista never got the opportunity to make the attack. Ringgold and Duncan cut swaths in the Mexican ranks, men falling in pieces as they were hit by shot, cannister or grape from the American cannon. Taylor ordered the

88

deadly 18-pound cannon to open fire, and the devastation increased.

The Mexicans were no match for the Americans. Their weapons were old and their powder defective. Most of their cannonballs fell short and bounced along the ground. They had no explosive shells. The Americans merely sidestepped them and continued the advance. The fight had begun about three o'clock in the afternoon, and the battlefield was quickly shrouded by smoke from the cannons and from the swatches of dry grass which had caught fire from the burning waddings of the cannon.

Believing that he could take advantage of the cover which the smoke would provide, General Torrejon dashed out leading a thousand lancers in an effort to flank Taylor's lines and attack the supply wagons at the rear. Twiggs's Fifth Infantry stood firm, the men pouring deadly musket fire into the horsemen. The lancers faltered, then wheeled about after Ringgold horsed his guns about to spray them with grapeshot. Taylor rushed the Second Dragoons into the fray, hoping to mount an attack. But the plans of both generals were scotched when a brisk wind fanned the grass fire into a smoky blaze which reduced visibility.

The cannonading ceased for a moment; then the coastal breezes whisked away the smoke and the battle resumed. During the lull, Taylor had moved his troops forward.

"Duncan's artillery poured into them a few rounds of grape and cannister and mowed them down in great numbers," Dr. Mills wrote. "His shells and shrapnel shot told with murderous effect," Captain Henry added. Duncan moved under the cover of the smoke screen to within 300 yards of the Mexicans, then bombarded them with telling effect.

Duncan was in field command of the artillery now. Ringgold had been mortally wounded when both of his legs were shot away by a Mexican cannonball. Duncan, standing erect in his stirrups, directed the gunfire. Taylor hoped to exploit the advantage with a mounted attack, but darkness closed over the battlefield and fighting ceased. It was about seven o'clock when the Americans were ordered to bivouac on the battlefield. The Mexicans had withdrawn a short distance and apparently settled down for the night.

With both forces bathed in full moonlight, the 56 American dead and wounded were collected. Arista lost at least 600 in dead and wounded, according to the American estimate.

"The surgeon's saw kept going all night, and the groans and screams from the improvised field hospital, where tobacco and brandy were the only palliatives, made sleeping difficult," one soldier wrote about the battle.

". . . I saw heads and limbs severed from their bodies and trunks strewed about in awful confusion. Many a body . . . had been cut in twain by our 18-pounders," Dr. Mills said. ". . . Such ghastly spectacles I hope never to behold again."

Though the losses inflicted on the enemy had been heavy, it was a psychological victory which mattered to Taylor. He had defeated a force superior in both men and arms to his tiny army. Taylor was extremely proud of his men and said so not only then but on many later occasions.

Taylor assumed that the battle would be rejoined at first light, and he had his men shaken awake before dawn. But as daylight melted away the night, Taylor was amazed to discover that the Mexicans had fled during the night, the last of them riding away as he scanned the battlefield. A lusty cheer went up from the American troops, and Taylor smiled broadly. The victory was even more complete than he had believed.

Taylor sent Captain Walker after the Mexicans to determine their future battle plans if he could. Walker returned with the report that the Mexicans appeared in full retreat toward the Rio Grande. Taylor discussed the situation with his senior officers, finding that they were eager to continue the fight. ". . . The General sided with them; his mind was doubtless made up beforehand," Holman Hamilton wryly observed.

But Taylor was cautious. Arista's withdrawal might be a trap. Taylor ordered the Dragoons to follow and observe, keeping out of range. Preparations to move ahead were then expedited, and Taylor wrote a detailed report to Washington about the battle.

Shortly after noon, Capt. George McCall sent word that the Mexicans were dug in at Resaca de la Palma ("ravine of the palms"), which was about five miles from Palo Alto. By two o'clock, Taylor was aboard Old Whitey and headed for the new battle area. Taylor had about 1,700 men with him.

General Arista had chosen a strong defensive point to contest Taylor's advance. It was an old riverbed with banks about four feet high. The bottom was cluttered with stumps, palm trees and pools of water of unknown depth. Dense chaparral, cactus and undergrowth blocked the passage on either side of the road to Matamoros. Arista seemed in command of the situation, being able to choose where a battle would be fought. It was a tactic which Taylor would use with great effectiveness later on, but he was faced with the problem now.

Taylor was certain that Arista had placed artillery to strafe the advancing Americans, but he couldn't locate them. Lieut. Stephen Decatur Dobbins was ordered forward with a small detachment of men to draw Mexican fire and expose their positions. The plan succeeded. As Dobbins' detachment rounded a curve in the road, they were "saluted with a shower of grapeshot which wounded him and two sergeants and killed a private." With the positions located, Taylor order Ringgold's battery, now commanded by Lieut. Randolph Ridgely, to attack. Infantry units were deployed to both right and left, and the fight was on.

Arista's command had been strengthened with reinforcements from Matamoros, and he was confident of success. The Mexican general retired to the shaded marquee of the gaudily decorated field tent to write some personal letters and listen to the military band concert which he had ordered to entertain him. Even when a courier breathlessly warned Arista that the Americans were coming, he ignored it. His subordinate officers had incorrectly estimated Taylor's losses, and Arista didn't think that Taylor could mount a successful attack.

Ridgely galloped down the road with his flying artillery. At a range of little more than 25 yards, the guns were swung about. The cannoneers wrestled the guns into firing position by hand. The six-pounders roared. Sweat trickled down the bare chests of the artillerymen as they rammed home powder, shot and shell, fired, then repeated the process. The gallant battery showered the enemy with such murderous fire that the Mexicans were forced to fall back. But Ridgely realized that he couldn't silence the Mexicans without support.

Taylor threw Captain May's Second Dragoons into the fight. May, his long, black beard and hair flowing out behind him, led his mounted riflemen up the road, with Taylor's command ringing in his ears: "Charge, Captain. Charge, *nolens volens*" ("willing or not").

May and Ridgely orchestrated their attack as the Mexicans shifted locations, trying to avoid the deadly fire being poured in on them. As May rode up to the artillery, Ridgely yelled: "Hold on, Charley, until I draw their fire."

May paused while the Mexicans directed their fire at Ridgely; then he waved his men to charge General de la Vega's emplacement. They actually overrode it as they fought through the enemy lines. May wheeled, then attacked from the rear and took several prisoners, including de la Vega, who was taken to Taylor for questioning.

May lost nine men killed and ten wounded in the assault, but the back of the Mexican defenses had been broken by his courageous, almost foolhardy charge. He was brevetted two grades following the battle.

The foot soldiers fought bravely and effectively. Capt. Phil Barbour's infantry company found an unused footpath, flanked the Mexicans and attacked from the rear. They captured cannons and forced the Rancheros cavalry (irregulars) to withdraw or face extinction. Lieutenant Grant led his men in another sector, capturing a colonel and other prisoners.

". . . My exploit was equal to that of the soldier who boasted that he had cut off the leg of one enemy," Grant wrote of his experiences. "When asked why he didn't cut off the head, he replied: 'Someone had done that before.'"

Though the cannons had broken through the defenses, the battle became hand-to-hand combat, with the soldiers making free use of the bayonet as they moved forward. When the Eighth Infantry faltered at the force of a counterattack, Taylor yelled: "Take those guns, and by God, keep them."

General Taylor sat on Old Whitey, his sword drawn, in the thickest of the fight while the musket balls rattled around him. A fellow officer commented that he was unnecessarily exposing himself, and suggested that Taylor withdraw a distance from the area.

"Let us ride a little nearer and the musket balls will then fall behind us," Taylor replied.

General Arista seemed to be in a trance about the battle. He sat in his long underwear composing a long report about the Mexican "victory" at Palo Alto. He sent his best units into impossible situations, committing them piecemeal so their numbers made no effective force. At last, convinced that the Americans were winning, Arista roused himself from his writing desk, ignored the groans and wailing of his wounded soldiers, cursed the others as cowards and fools, then ordered the bugler to sound retreat. He took command of a cavalry unit and galloped off toward the Rio Grande. The infantry was already on the road. Once at the river, the Mexicans tried to launch boats they found moored to the shore. But the frightened, exhausted men overloaded them, and many were thrown into the muddy water. Cavalrymen rode their horses into some of the boats, upsetting them. Men and animals were bobbing in the water, the number in sight diminishing as they were swept away or sank below the surface. Gunfire from men of Fort Texas picked at the stragglers until it seemed that the Rio Grande would run red with Mexican blood, and the retreat became a massacre.

Arista only officially admitted to 160 dead, 228 wounded and another 159 missing, but the real figures were much higher. American officers estimated that 1,500 casualties must have been nearer the true figure from the battle and the river disaster. Even so, the Americans had gained a respect for the fight. "The enemy fought like devils," Capt. E. Kirby Smith said.

General Taylor would have agreed on that. He reported that three officers and 36 enlisted men had been killed, and 89 more wounded. There was no doubt, however, that Taylor had won a smashing one-sided victory.

". . . I think you will find that history will count the victory just achieved as one of the greatest on record," Lieutenant Grant wrote somewhat ingenuously to his sweetheart. Taylor was enormously pleased and praised his men fulsomely for their "coolness and readiness." They had defeated a trained army three times their size, and had captured an impressive amount of booty, including General Arista's solid gold dining service and his personal correspondence, much of which was devoted to his descriptions of the victories over the Americans.

General Taylor might have crossed the river and forced Arista to either fight or surrender his entire army. But it wasn't Taylor's nature to act precipitously. Besides, the pontoon bridges which he had requested from Washington months before had not arrived. Without them a hurried crossing would have been needlessly hazardous.

Despite Taylor's firsthand knowledge of conditions and bloody proof that his military judgment was sound in the first two battles, there were armchair critics in far-off Washington who carped at General Taylor for not finishing off the Mexicans. No one considered that Taylor's men were exhausted and his supplies low. To Taylor, knowing that, the argument ended at that point.

Fort Texas had easily sustained the siege of Mexican shelling. Only two casualties had been suffered. One of them was Major Jacob Brown, who was killed. The fort was immediately renamed in his honor and became the site of Brownsville, Texas.

With the situation well in hand, General Taylor rode off to confer with Commodore Conners about logistic problems which might arise as the campaign continued and widened in scope. From this meeting, the "incident of the uniform" arose.

Conners was a "spit-and-polish" officer, being fond of outward signs of rank and honors. In deference to his attitude, Taylor dug his wrinkled full-dress uniform out of his foot locker, along with a sash, sword, epaulettes and regalia of a brigadier general. Conners, who knew Taylor's attitude and liked him for his love of ease and informality, decided to wear his most casual clothes for the meeting. When the men met aboard Conners's ship, they first stared at one another, then broke into a laugh, pointing to the uniform of the other. It made their meeting even more pleasant, and Taylor vowed that he would never again wear a full-dress uniform for such meetings—any meeting, for that matter.

Taylor arranged for a shipment of ammunition and supplies, then returned to Fort Brown on May 13. Awaiting him was a proposal from General Arista suggesting an armistice between the armies while they awaited the outcome of negotiations taking place in Mexico City. Taylor's refusal was firm and explicit:

". . . I must have Matamoros even if I am forced to batter down the town," he wrote in reply. "And I am fully prepared to do just that thing. These are my terms: the city must capitulate; all property surrendered; then, and only then, may the Mexican army march out and retire. . . ."

Taylor expected a delaying answer of some kind from the enemy, but he didn't sit idly by waiting for it. A detachment was ordered to seize Burrita, about 15 miles south of Matamoros. From there patrols moved across the river and stole boats, which the assault troops would use to make the attack on Matamoros. The boats were moored below Fort Brown, out of Mexican range.

General Arista didn't underestimate Taylor's ability or intentions this time. He sent General Requeña to discuss the matter with Taylor, but no agreement was reached. Taylor repeated his intention to shell the city into rubble unless it surrendered on his terms.

Secretly, Arista ordered all cannons spiked and ammunition pitched into the river. Then, at night, he led his troops out of Matamoros toward Linares. Behind him, Arista left 300 wounded and disabled soldiers in the overcrowded and poorly equipped hospitals. The men were abandoned virtually unattended.

American scouts reported that Arista had fled, but Taylor wasn't content to accept unconfirmed reports when the safety of his men was at stake. The 18-pound siege guns were moved into position to cover a river crossing. Captain Walker and ten Rangers moved across the Rio Grande to make a final reconnaissance. Meanwhile, the six-pound cannons had been dismounted from their carriages and loaded into the boats. The First Infantry landed just below Matamoros, and they had advanced but a short distance when they were met, not by Mexican gunfire as expected but a delegation of residents, all of them dressed in white and all carrying white flags. They offered to surrender the city.

. . "The scare of the terrible Yankee wrath was still working," Captain Henry remarked.

Captain May led his Second Dragoons into Matamoros to lower the Mexican flag and replace it with the Stars and Stripes.

Taylor ordered camp be pitched outside of the city limits and assigned Colonel Twiggs to supervise and patrol the Matamoros. Troops were permitted within the city in limitod numbers at first, and were warned that any looting or mistreatment of the civilians would be severely punished. Taylor did allow confiscation of tobacco which had been intended for Mexican troops, but nothing else was officially liberated.

Lieut. Col. John Garland led a detachment of Dragoons in pursuit of Arista's fleeing troops to harass them if possible. No military contact was made, but Garland was able to report evidence of a frantic flight—wounded men abandoned to their fate, discarded weapons and other supplies thrown carelessly by the side of the road. Arista made a forced march through blistering heat, then drenching rain. Men died of sunstroke, exhaustion, even suicide—many of them being unwilling to continue the death march. Less than half of Arista's original command marched into Linares. It was a military disaster of the first magnitude for the Mexicans.

Garland returned to Matamoros with 22 prisoners, along with a great deal of valuable military intelligence about the route to Linares. His estimate was that Mexico could not be

safely invaded via Linares because of the uncertain supply
lines and the difficulty of the route. His report was later confirmed when Maj. Ben McCullough made a reconnaisance of
the Linares route, then the interior through Camargo via
the Rio Grande. Taylor favored the advance through Camargo, and the decision was made when McCullough's report was received.

". . . A survey of the field action and of this country . . .
proved that the Mexicans were totally and completely
routed," Lieutenant Meade wrote following an inspection
patrol, "and the defeat could not have been more complete,
except that we had not the men to pursue the fugitives and
make them prisoners. . . ."

Matamoros, a city of about 8,000, was a fine prize, though
a disappointment to many of the American soldiers, who
found that the dark-skinned girls they had seen from across
the river were something quite different when viewed close
at hand. Lieutenant Meade said " they were the most miser-
able-looking señoritas," they were "nothing but old hags,
worse-looking than the Indians."

General Taylor wasn't disappointed, however. He had
won his first two battles, and his son Richard, who had graduated from Yale in 1845, was among the victorious soldiers,
having come through unscathed. Seated in front of his tent
pitched outside Matamoros, Taylor, dressed in Attakapas
pantaloons and a linen roundabout, with a straw hat
jammed down on his head, wrote his orders and reports
using two blue-painted chests for a desk. Amid the confusion of official reports and papers, Taylor studied the strategy of the war ahead and wondered when Washington
would reply to his requests for continuing the conquest of
Mexico. When visitors were received, Taylor would shout
for his orderly, Ben, who would instantly appear with a tin
tray bearing a pair of whiskey bottles, tumblers and an
earthen pitcher which contained some of the honey-colored

water from the Rio Grande. When ice was finally shipped to Matamoros, juleps and other coolers became feasible.

"A long step toward civilization," wrote George W. Kendall, war correspondent for the *New Orleans Picayune.*

Nine

GETTING SET

General Taylor had sent a dispatch to Washington saying "hostilities may now have been considered as commenced" following the ambush of Captain Thornton's troops. But it was not until two weeks later that the news reached President Polk. Transmission of information was absurdly slow between Taylor's and Polk's offices. The dispatches moved either by courier on horseback or, sometimes, by ship. The lagging line of communication was responsible for many misunderstandings between the army and the President.

Even before he knew that blood had already been spilled, President Polk polled his Cabinet about a declaration of war. All approved except Secretary of Navy George Bancroft, who said he could agree only if there were any overt acts by the Mexicans. Later that same day, May 9, President Polk was handed Taylor's dispatches telling of the Thornton massacre. The President reassembled his Cabinet at 7:30 P.M. to take up the issue of war and peace. This time the vote was unanimous for an immediate declaration of war. Polk had moved cautiously, he believed: "We will not be the aggressors."

Secretary of State Buchanan pointed out that the President "is ready to present the olive branch to Mexico the moment he knows it will be accepted."

But the thought of conciliation was gone now. President Polk gave a ringing challenge in his message to Congress: "The Mexicans shed American blood upon American soil. War exists by the act of Mexico itself."

Though he regretted breaking the sabbath, the President worked on Sunday to prepare his war message for Congress, which included a $10,000,000 appropriation and request for 50,000 men to flesh out the army. Substantially there were four reasons for the war—the annexation of Texas; the Texas-Mexico boundary dispute over the area situated between the Rio Grande and Nueces rivers; the rejection of Ambassador John Sliddel; and, finally, the settlement of various damage claims by the Americans arising out of the Texas revolution.

Opponents claimed that President Polk wanted to be a war president. He also wanted to enhance the Democratic Party with the prestige of crushing Mexico in a quick, inexpensive war, they said. Other critics added that the war was a result of pressure from Southerners seeking new slave states, which would increase Southern influence.

There was heated, acrimonious debate in both Houses of Congress as the war message was considered. The House passed it, 173 to 14. After studying the measure for an additional 24 hours, the Senate concurred, 42 to 2.

On the next day, May 14, 1846, Secretary Buchanan said: "We go to war with Mexico solely for the purpose of conquering an honorable and just peace. Whilst we intend to prosecute the war with vigor, both by land and sea, we shall bear the olive branch in one hand, and the sword in the other; and whenever she will accept the former, we shall sheath the latter."

The United States was woefully unprepared. Incredibly, other than moving Taylor into a provocative situation as an Army of Observation and Occupation, Polk had done nothing whatever to prepare the nation for a full-scale war. First,

a commanding general for the phantom army had to be
named; then moves could be made to field troops.

The first choice was Maj. Gen. Winfield Scott, ranking
army officer, called "Old Fuss and Feathers" because of his
purse-mouthed attention to trifling details of military matters. Scott, 60 years old, was a brave, skillful officer with
many years of command experience, and he was commanding general of the entire U.S. Army. Polk hesitated about ap-
pointing Scott, because he knew the soldier was politically
ambitious. Scott, an ardent Whig, had received 39 votes toward the presidential nomination at the 1839 convention.
Polk, a narrow, partisan Democrat, was reluctant about ele-
vating a potential political opponent who might vault from
war hero to the presidency. But Polk's alternative choice
was General Taylor, also a Whig. Though he seemed to be
the safer selection because of his lack of political ambition
and his oft-stated desire to retire, Polk was skeptical about
Taylor's command qualities and knew nothing about the first
two military victories at the time.

Believing that, in all fairness, Scott at least deserved a
chance, Polk appointed him to command all land operations
against Mexico on the day war was declared. There were
personality and policy clashes from the outset.

Polk assumed that Scott would take immediate field command. Scott planned to stay in Washington until fall, when
the fever threat was over and he would have more troops.
Polk pointed out that many volunteers would have spent
most of their enlistment marking time in the United States.
Scott shrugged, continued to solve logistics problems and
study the available maps, most of which had been drawn
with more optimism than accuracy. Polk's anger mounted as
Scott remained serene and aloof. The President considered
Scott's procrastination to be a political plot to extend the
war and discredit the Democrats! Polk publicly described

Scott's ideas as "scientific and visionary," and stated that further delay would not be tolerated.

Scott blundered with a remark that he didn't wish to be placed in that most undesirable position of being where he would be fired on by the Mexicans from the front, and by the politicians in Washington from the rear. Scott's hauteur collapsed when he was superseded in field command by Taylor after the President learned of the victories achieved by Old Rough and Ready. Taylor was brevetted to major general for "gallant conduct and distinguished services in the successive victories over superior Mexican forces." Taylor now ranked with Scott, who would remain in Washington. Taylor would command the field troops.

Scott realized that he had committed military suicide with a goose quill. Then he compounded the error by writing Polk to apologize for his remarks, which had been composed while having a "hasty plate of soup," another unfortunate statement. One Washington wit dubbed Scott "Marshal Tureen," an oblique reference to the tureen of soup.

"Mexico or Death" became the rallying cry of the nation as war hysteria mounted, and volunteers responded eagerly. Tennessee had 30,000 volunteers to fill a 3,000-man quota. North Carolina recruited three times the number of required men. Lew Wallace, later a general and author of *Ben Hur*, then only 19, personally recruited a company of soldiers from his fellow law students in Indianapolis. Ohioans, who had generally opposed the acquisition of Texas, had 3,000 men ready within hours after the first sign "For Mexico, Fall In" appeared.

The federal plan was to draw most of the combat volunteers from the areas in which the expansionist and war feelings ran highest—Georgia, Alabama, Mississippi, Tennessee, Kentucky, Ohio, Indiana, Illinois, Missouri, Arkansas and Texas. Men from other states were held on a ready-reserve

basis. Though there might be some national doubt about
Polk's wisdom or motives, there was no question about support or patriotism when the United States was threatened.

While the war fever sparked everyone, General Taylor remained singularly unimpressed with being given command
of the interior campaign. "I heartily wish the war was at an
end," he said.

But neither the public nor the politicians were going to
permit the first hero of the Mexican War to remain unsung
and unrewarded, even though there were some grave doubts
among military people about Taylor's ability to manage such
a command.

Congress authorized the stamping of a gold medallion,
though it had to be delayed because there was no likeness of
Taylor available. A Louisiana legislature voted a jeweled
sword, plus a military sash once owned by General Washington to be given Taylor. Newborn sons were being named
Zachary. Most significant was the statement by Thurlow
Weed, a power in Whig politics and editor of the *Albany
Journal*, who flatly predicted Taylor's election to the Presidency as soon as the war was won! Polk's somewhat kinky
temper curled further with the talk that Taylor might be a
political opponent.

In the face of it all, Taylor remained calm. He wrote his
son-in-law, Dr. Wood: ". . . They need have no apprehensions of being interfered with by men for that high office,
which I would decline if proffered & I could reach it without opposition." Taylor continued to express his political reluctance for many months to come, though the chance for
the greatest possible political prize finally became too entic-
ing.

If Taylor was flattered by any comment, it was the
printed statement of an anonymous trooper, which said, in
part: ". . . During all of the battles, General Taylor headed
his troops in the most cool and gallant manner. His escape

from hurt seems almost a miracle. He has won the hearts of his soldiers by his willingness to share with them the iminent perils. His motto is 'I wish no man to go where I am not willing to lead.' He has, indeed, been 'Old Rough & Ready.'. . ."

Taylor easily won the respect and admiration of his men for many reasons. Though he didn't approve of roistering and other earthy delights in which his men engaged in Matamoros, he often looked away. Men faced with combat were entitled to some comforts. In his tented headquarters outside Matamoros, while he waited for further orders to advance, he listened to complaints or items of official business with equal interest, and was approachable by all.

"He will sit and talk with the commonest soldier in the most affable manner," one disabled soldier commented after he was invalided home. "He will enter minutely into the private affairs of the soldiers under his command, give them his advice when asked, as it frequently is, and when that is over, read to them from the newspapers the anecdotes about the army, which have made their way into print in the northern cities, at which he would laugh as heartily as any of them."

As a result, Taylor's men were inordinately loyal, and when they were ordered out of his command, tears were not uncommon.

With fighting in prospect and little other than routine duty to engage them, Taylor's men often became restless and beset by difficulties. Matamoros was heavily seeded with taverns and gambling deadfalls, places where trouble always blossoms. Regulars, volunteers and especially the Texas Rangers engaged in all manner of mischief. When they could find no other excitement, they fought each other, often with sanguinary results.

A Mexican girl was bayonetted because she was tardy in serving drinks. A Ranger shot an actor on the stage because he didn't approve of the performance, then simply "sloped away" without ever being caught. Several soldiers were badly wounded following a brawl over a catfish, and numerous other troubles erupted. But conditions bettered as some of the short-time volunteers were discharged and Taylor's tiny army melted down to a hard core of tough troops.

Interminably slow communications delayed Taylor, but he believed that the next major move would be toward Monterrey and began to take steps towards shaping that strategy. Captain McCullough reported the best military route was through Camargo, about 130 miles upstream at a point where the San Juan River emptied into the Rio Grande.

Lacking enough boats to move troops, cannons and baggage upriver, Taylor sent a procurement officer back to the United States to purchase suitable boats. Then he moved ahead with planning the attack, even though there was still no word about over-all strategy or about the changing scene in Washington.

Taylor sent 300 infantrymen and Texas Rangers, supported by artillery, to capture the village of Reynosa, about 60 miles from Matamoros. The seizure was made without resistance. The resident Mexicans were actually pleased with the change of command. Mexican General Canales and his irregular Ranchero cavalry had been living off residents of the village and literally eating them out of house and home. Not long afterwards, Taylor had gathered enough river boats to begin a move against Camargo.

Late rains had raised the level of the river, but Taylor's men managed the boats skillfully. "The Rio Grande is a noble river at this stage of water," Captain Barbour wrote. "There is not a snag in it. . . . The Mexicans appear to be exceedingly friendly along the river."

Many of the troops had moved upstream by the time Taylor and his headquarters staff boarded the *Hatchee Eagle* on August 4. The men who had been forced to march found the going both difficult and disagreeable.

"The heat was intense, and the men suffered very much," Captain Henry said. "I am free to confess, had not my pride come to the rescue, I would have given out. . . ."

When feasible, the troops moved at night, because during the day the ground was so hot that the men's feet burned. Dense chaparral blocked the sea breezes which cooled some sections. But they eventually completed the arduous march and reached Camargo, as did Taylor, who moored there August 8, 1846. Camargo was a wretched town of about 3,000 residents. Though militarily Camargo was ideal as a base and supply point to support Taylor's march into the interior, it was otherwise a pest hole. The San Juan River had overflowed and devastated a large section of the town. The town's water supply was contaminated; mosquitoes teemed in the stagnant ponds and sanitation was almost unknown. The men fell ill with diarrhea and dysentery, along with assorted other ailments common to troops in strange environments. Those who didn't become ill had brought their immunity with them.

"Camargo is the sickliest place I think in the world," Gen. Gideon Pillow wrote, "and it is only a matter of surprise and wonder that I am still alive. I suppose we must have buried a thousand poor volunteers. . . ."

Pillow, a goateed, energetic, intelligent and handsome man, was a political general who lacked military experience. He had been made a member of Taylor's command because he had been a former law partner of President Polk. Pillow was a severe critic of Taylor and did his best to discredit Taylor throughout their association. It is not unlikely that Pillow might have been assigned to act as an observer sub rosa for Polk.

"What a horror I have for Camargo," another officer wrote. "It is a Yawning Grave Yard. . . ."

As usual, the soldiers took advantage of what diversions they could find. With 11,000 men assembled in a village able to accomodate a fourth of that number under optimum con-

ditions, the guardhouses were usually crammed to capacity
too. "The volunteers are playing the Devil and disgracing
our country," one officer said. Taylor described the Texas
Rangers' conduct as "licentious," but he stolidly continued
to map plans for the march toward Monterrey.

Meanwhile, in Washington, President Polk was tinkering
on the diplomatic front, still hoping that the war could be
settled quickly without extended conflict and loss of life. His
hopes must have clouded his judgment. Polk became the
dupe in one of the most absurd intrigues which ever embroiled the United States, a case which included many egregious diplomatic errors.

Through unofficial channels, Polk had been contacted by
that master schemer Antonio Lopez de Santa Anna, who
hinted that a peaceful solution to the war might be found,
provided that he was well paid and returned to power as
president, an office which he held many times. Polk snapped
at the lure, like a trout for a fly, even though advisers
warned him about Santa Anna, a known knave.

Santa Anna was born in Jalapa, Mexico, in 1794 of
wealthy parents, and from his teens had evidenced a pre-
dilection for intrigue, gambling and gaudy uniforms, all of
which thrust him into the center of attention. He had obtained a fine education and was a skilled officer. Santa Anna
was President of Mexico in 1832 and again briefly in 1840.
He had lost a leg fighting against the French in Vera Cruz,
and had the severed limb enshrined in a crystal urn and
placed atop a monument. But when Santa Anna again fell
from favor, which he frequently did, mobs disinterred the
grisly object and dragged it through the streets. In 1846
Santa Anna was in exile in Havana, Cuba, but was anxious
to return home.

The Parades government was tottering in public favor,
owing partly to the President's heavy drinking. Santa Anna
suggested to Polk that he could overthrow the present re-

gime if Polk would provide official permission to pass through the American naval blockade. Santa Anna said he would need $30,000,000 to pay off Church obligations, wages due soldiers, bribes and other debts. Santa Anna expected to keep about $1,000,000 for himself. But in exchange for his efforts, Santa Anna would cede all of the territory sought by the United States, including Texas and California!

Polk was skeptical but became convinced that Santa Anna would prove to be so disruptive in Mexico, even if he didn't fulfill his promises to the Americans, that Polk's goals would be achieved anyway. Polk sent Commander Alexander Sliddel Mackenzie to Cuba to explore the situation. Not long afterwards, Navy Secretary Bancroft instructed Commodore Conners: "If General Santa Anna endeavors to enter the Mexican ports you will allow him to pass freely."

On August 12, 1846, the British steamer *Arab* sailed through the naval blockade at Vera Cruz. Aboard was the self-styled Napoleon of the West and his handsome child bride, called "The Flower of Mexico," who were returning to Mexico from Cuban exile. Though an English newspaper disparaged the return of Santa Anna as "that very sorry hero but most determined cockfighter," the Mexican populace was jubilant with his triumphal return. Bells tolled and cannons boomed their salutes. Like the buccaneers of old, Santa Anna quickly unfurled his true colors as soon as it was safe for him to do so. To the sound of Te Deums in the background, Santa Anna publicly appointed himself as commander in chief of the Mexican "Army of Liberation," whose slogan was: "Federation, Santa Anna and Texas."

Despite his pride in scheming and intrigue, Polk had been completely outsmarted by "Old Peg Leg," as Santa Anna was affectionately called by his troops. He immediately levied heavy taxes on the Catholic Church and all merchants, then called for 30,000 troops to be assembled at San

Luis Potosí. From that base, 380 miles away, Santa Anna planned to direct the fight in the northern sector of Mexico. Polk's scheming had managed to provide Mexico with the best possible military officer to face Zach Taylor's little army!

"Everyday that passes without fighting at the north is a century of disgrace for Mexico," Santa Anna said in a fiery speech. He had the further advantages of knowing that President Polk and General Taylor were operating in separate vacuums, neither knowing exactly what the other was doing because of the lag in communications and mutual distrust.

Taylor divided his command into two regular divisions. Twiggs, now a general, would command the First Division, and Worth the Second Division. A segment of volunteers from Texas would be led by Gen. Pinkney Henderson, and another group of volunteers from Ohio, Kentucky, Tennessee and Mississippi would be led by Gen. William O. Butler. Gen. Robert Patterson was left in command of the several thousand men who were disabled or otherwise unfit for combat, and stationed at Matamoros, Camargo or other posts.

Worth's Second Division was the first unit to leave Camargo and head toward Monterrey. It was August 19. It wasn't until the first week in September that all of Taylor's 6,640 men cleared the pest-ridden city. Taylor informed Washington of his strategy and the forces he expected to meet en route to Monterrey.

Polk, blatantly ignoring the fact that Taylor had fought the war entirely on his own initiative, wrote in his diary: "General Taylor, I fear, is not the man for the command of the army. He is brave but does seem to have the resources or grasp of mind enough to conduct such a campaign. . . . Though this is so, I know of no one whom I can put in his place. . . ."

Naturally, General Taylor was unaware of the carping comment and probably wouldn't have cared anyway. He was concerned with the forthcoming meeting with the Mexicans in what might become a decisive battle at Monterrey. He was concerned, too, because of Santa Anna's return and the intelligence which indicated that the Mexican general was training a strong force to fight him. The reports were not clear as to where the confrontation might be made.

Whatever doubts he might have entertained were dispelled when, on September 19, 1846, artillery fire greeted the advancing American troops as they drew within sight of Monterrey.

The first cannonball whizzed within ten feet of Taylor. Two other projectiles whistled through the ranks of the soldiers, miraculously not harming a man.

There was going to be a defense of Monterrey. No doubt about that.

Ten

BATTLE OF MONTERREY

General Taylor withdrew beyond artillery range to consider the capture of the armed city. He scanned Monterrey through glasses as he slouched in the saddle, one leg hooked over the pommel in a characteristic attitude.

Monterrey was obviously a strongly fortified city. Built in the old Spanish style, it was surrounded by massive stone walls which were supplemented with ditches, bastions and towers. The houses were stone or adobe, mostly of one story in height, but the cathedrals and public buildings, like most of those throughout Mexico, were large and imposing.

General Ampudia had planned the defense carefully. Not only were the walls and parapets lined with cannon, but the houses bristled with riflemen. The streets were barricaded and planted with artillery in such a way that any approach could be swept clear with cannon fire.

The Santa Caterina River ran through the city's outskirts, and the road which led to Saltillo followed its course. Monterrey, it seemed, had to be approached across an open plain which was commanded by a strong fortification called the Black Fort—an unfinished church whose weather-blackened walls sprouted ten cannons. The entire plain was planted with various crops, which might provide some cover for advancing troops, but the area was exposed enough that it could be swept by cross fire from the emplaced cannon. To the rear and on both sides of Monterrey stood two high strong points which Taylor realized would be difficult to overcome.

One was Federation Hill, which stood across the river. from the eastern edge of the city. It was a sheer, high eminence, well fortified with a fort called El Soldado, which contained at least two nine-pound cannons.

On the western approach stood Independence Hill, which was fortified on top by the Bishop's Palace, and below by a smaller redoubt, El Obispado. With the city walled and guarded with fortified high points on either flank, there was only an open approach in a frontal assault. Taylor knew he faced a difficult, perhaps bloody fight for Monterrey, but there was no avoiding it.

To confirm his observations, Taylor sent out scouts to study the Mexicans' defenses. Happily, they discovered that Monterrey was poorly guarded from the rear. They believed that the city might be flanked and attacked from the rear, while a military demonstration was being made at the front to draw attention.

Within Monterrey, Ampudia circulated pamphlets, dated September 14, 1846, which called upon his soldiers to display their true valor and courage in the forthcoming fight. He assured them that the enemy would be soundly and quickly defeated. Ampudia's closing statement was: "Soldiers—victory or death must be our only device."

Ampudia tried to convince Taylor's men that a fight was futile by calling: "We are waiting for you! If you join us, you will receive lands and rewards according to your rank." It was an appeal similar to the one which had worked at Matamoros, inducements which had caused John Riley and others to defect. Some of those deserters were among the defenders of Monterrey. But there were no more defections among the Americans.

Taylor bivouacked at Walnut Springs, a grove of pecan trees shaggy with Spanish moss; several cold springs bubbled up nearby. As night closed in on that Saturday, September 19, Taylor could see the city light up and he could hear the faint notes of the strident Mexican bugles.

During the afternoon, patrols of Texans, heavily armed with Colt pistols and rifles and colorfully dressed in buckskins, red shirts and felt hats, had nabbed three Mexicans spying on the Americans. After "chafing them a bit" the Texans extracted valuable information for battle strategy. Acting on this information, Taylor split his forces, ordering General Worth's Second Division to flank Independence Hill and attack from the rear. Taylor assigned Captain Mackall's and Lieutenant Duncan's artillery and Texas Rangers commanded by Col. Jack Hays and Sam Walks to move with Worth. In all there would be 2,200 men.

Taylor was awakened that night by a huge wavering light. He peered out to see that all of the crops—grain, cotton and sugar cane—which grew on the plain were aflame. Taylor smiled. Ampudia was obviously expecting a frontal attack. He had a surprise for him.

It was two o'clock in the afternoon of September 20 before Worth took up the line of march. Captain Sanders and Lieutenant Meade reported that the Mexicans had discovered the plan and were strengthening forces at the Bishop's Palace. Worth continued the flanking movement, keeping just out of range of Mexican cannons. About the same time, Twiggs' First Division and Butler's volunteers began a feinting attack toward the front of Monterrey. Two 24-pound howitzers and a ten-inch mortar were moved up to lob shells into the city and provide another diversion to help Worth's attack.

A light rain began to fall before dark. Having gone about seven miles, Worth ordered that camp be pitched. By the light of burning corn husks, Worth scribbled a dispatch advising Taylor that the attack on Independence Hill would be launched at dawn and asked all diversions possible—a request which Taylor had anticipated.

Because of the oppressive heat during the march, most of the soldiers had thrown away their rations to save the weight. Skimpy meals were made from a few ducks and chickens which the soldiers had been able to liberate from the Mexicans after they camped.

Those soldiers able to sleep were shaken awake at dawn, and the division was put into motion. In the distance they could hear the rumble of Taylor's guns beginning the diversionary bombardment.

Contact was made immediately with the Mexican cavalrymen. With their lances flashing, they charged the 400 Texans led by Colonel Hays. For a moment neither adversary gave an inch. Lances probed and the heavy "wrist breaker" sabers of the mounted Americans slashed. Riflemen sowed the air with musket balls. By main force, the Texans aboard heavier horses bowled over the lighter, smaller Mexican mustangs, throwing off the riders and blunting the point of the attack. The Texans worked quickly and savagely with pistol, rifle, sabre or lance and the Mexicans began to withdraw. Before they could regroup, Duncan's flying artillery rattled up and showers of grape and cannister scattered the Mexicans. Horses reared and shrill whinnies split the air as the Mexicans retreated, leaving about a hundred dead and wounded behind. They galloped down the road to Saltillo.

The Texans' casualties were one dead, two wounded!

"The town is ours," Worth wrote Taylor, an estimate which proved to be extremely premature. Worth had cut the Saltillo road, a key objective which would deny the Mexicans reinforcements or supplies. But there were strong points to be overcome, and Monterrey was still intact.

As Worth's men emerged into the open, cannon fire rained down on them from Federation Hill across the river. They

were safe from the guns on Independence Hill above them
because the cannons couldn't be depressed far enough. The
men sought cover from the shelling. Rangers moved out on
the road to offset any surprise attack mounted from Saltillo.
Worth could hear the rumble of Taylor's guns as he ordered
six companies of dismounted Texans, supported by four
units of artillery, to mount an assault on Federation Hill
across the river. The Fifth and Seventh Infantries were to be
held as support and reserve units in the attack.

The military equation facing Taylor seemed equally simple, but scouts had made a tragic error in estimating the enemy's strength and in assessing their determination to stand
and fight. When he was certain that Worth was attacking,
Taylor called Lieutenant Colonel Garland:

"Colonel, lead the head of your column off to the left,
keeping well out of range of the enemy's guns, but if you
think you can take any of the little forts with bayonets,
you'd better do it."

Garland led the charge of the First and Third Washington
Volunteers toward a redoubt called Teneria, walking directly into a "saturnalia of slaughter." The men, like inno-
cents before a firing squad, were dazed and decimated, but
Garland managed to withdraw them in an orderly manner.
Taylor then threw the Fourth Infantry against Teneria, believing it could be overwhelmed. But the soldiers were
scythed down, 30 per cent of the troops falling dead or
wounded.

". . . We rushed into the streets," Captain Henry wrote,
"and had advanced but a short distance when we came suddenly upon an unknown battery which opened deadly fire
upon us. . . . On every side we were cut down. Major Barbour fell cheering his men. . . ."

Lieutenant Grant tried to rally his company of Fourth Infantrymen, but most of the survivors wandered dazed and
aimlessly through the streets. Informed of the situation, Tay-

lor rushed reinforcements in to rescue the men and capture
Teneria. Col. Jeff Davis, riding his favorite horse, Pompey,
arrived leading the Mississippi Rifles, surveyed the disaster,
then yelled: "Now is the time. Great God, if I had fifty men
with knives I could take that fort."

Pointing his sword toward the objective, the men
swarmed into the redoubt, followed by the Tennessee Volunteers. The Mexicans were short on ammunition. Some of
the sandbags covers were on fire and their casualties had
been heavy, but still they resisted the Americans.

"The combat began to be terrible," one Mexican officer
said. "The Americans, kneeling, concealing themselves in
every sort of posture within pistol shot, maintained a lively
fire."

The Mississippians and the Tennessee Volunteers continued to swarm over the parapets and Teneria fell into American hands.

"Three cheers for Old Zach," one enthusiastic Tennes-
seean yelped. Another volunteer said: "I was within ten feet
of General Taylor in Monterrey on the 21st. He was cool as
a cucumber and ordered us to pass into the city and break
open the houses. God knows how any of us got out."

The bitter house-to-house battle continued, the soldiers
battering doors down with planks, then breaking through
walls and roofs to seek and destroy snipers. Casualties
mounted, with nearly 400 officers and enlisted men killed or
wounded. But Ampudia was in the middle of a giant pin-
cers, which was being applied by Taylor on one side and
Worth on the other. Ampudia's strategy was to fight fiercely,
hoping to gain the best possible armistice terms. From the
beginning, the Mexicans seemed doomed to lose.

"Taylor's did the work, and our losses were Worth's gain,"
one subordinate officer commented. "With us judgment and
energy were quietly and surely advancing. On the other
side, Taylor's impetuosity and fearlessness showed a deter-

mination at all sacrifices to carry everything before them."
While Taylor was fighting in the streets, Capt. C. F. Smith
was leading his men across the river, all of them holding
their muskets or Hall carbines above their heads as they
splashed through the icy water. Once ashore, they rushed
for cover in the rocks and brush as the Mexicans moved to
the brow of the hill to repulse the attack. The foot soldiers
inched their way up the hill, while Capt. D. S. Mills led
reinforcements across the river. Cannon fire whooshed harm-
lessly over their heads, but the individual fire fight heated
up. The Mexicans upset their nine-pounder and panicked.
The Americans swarmed over the crest, righted the cannon
and turned it on the fleeing Mexicans. As they disappeared,
the cannons fired on Independence Hill, which was being attacked by part of Worth's command.

Independence Hill was a formidable objective. Its slopes
were sheer or composed of loose rock, which made footing
hazardous. Mexicans zeroed in on the advancing Americans,
who slipped and stumbled trying to ascend the eminence.
Rocks rolled down, and the rain sluiced the men and the
mountain. Worth's troops were only halfway up the hill
when night closed in, leaving the Americans to cling on the
precipitous hill for the night. There they stayed, cold, hungry and drenched with rain.

"Forward" was the whispered command at 3 A.M., and
the men responded eagerly. All were anxious to move after
the wretched night. Weapons in hand, the soldiers slipped
and clambered up the hill, their early charge surprising the
Mexicans. Up, up they moved through rocks and undergrowth, then over the ramparts, fighting hand to hand, bayonet to gullet or even with stones in hand when weapons were
lost in the fray. The Mexicans were forced off the hill, and
the Stars and Stripes fluttered over the Mexican fort, while
men of Taylor's command watched by the early morning
light:

". . . Just as the gray dawn of the day began, I witnessed the storming of the height," Captain Henry said. "The first intimation we had of it was the discharge of musketry near the top of Independence Hill. Each flash looked like an electric spark. The flashes and the white smoke ascended the hill gradually, as if worked by machinery. The dark space between the apex of the height and the curling smoke of the musketry became less and less, until the whole became enveloped in smoke, and we knew it was gallantly carried. It was a glorious sight, and quite warmed up our cold and chilled bodies.

Captain Henry was right. Monterrey now lay open from the west to be squeezed against Taylor's hard-fighting troops. Worth had accomplished it with only 32 dead and wounded, a remarkably light casualty list.

Only routine patrol activity was continued the next day, but on Wednesday the pressure was applied by both Taylor and Worth advancing from opposite sides of the city. Ampudia was surrounded in the plaza at the center of Monterrey, with virtually no chance to get out; but Taylor took no chances either. Artillery was moved into place, and the foot soldiers moved cautiously from house to house, pressing toward the plaza area. There were pockets of resistance, and both Mexicans and Americans continued to fall.

At a critical moment, ammunition ran low and Lieutenant Grant became a hero:

". . . I volunteered to go back to the point we had started from, report our position to Gen. Twiggs and ask for ammunition to be forwarded. . . . My ride back was an exposed one. . . . I adjusted myself on the side of the horse farthest from the enemy, on foot holding to the cantle of the saddle and an arm over the neck of the horse, I started at a full run. It was only at street crossings that my horse was under fire, but these I crossed at such a flying rate that generally I was past and under the cover of the next block of houses be-

fore the enemy fired. I got out safely without a scratch."
Taylor was entirely casual about the dangers of sniper fire
in the street fighting and strolled about, calmly issuing orders as he watched the progress of the battle. Worth's tactics, on the other side of the city, were substantially the
same—breaking into houses, walls and roofs to gain the high
points. Axes crashed, rifles cracked, men yelled and timbers
fell as the fight went on. The dead lay where they fell; the
wounded screamed in agony, or begged pitifully for water
or aid. Some hobbled away using muskets for crutches.

The fighting continued until nightfall, and even then shells
were lobbed into the Mexican sector. By Thursday, Ampudia was anxious to surrender. Col. Francisco Moreno
brought a letter from the commanding general. Couched in
flowery language, Ampudia said, in part: ". . . Having made
the defense of which I believe this city is susceptible, I have
fulfilled my duty, and have satisfied the military honor
[and] to prosecute the defense therefore would only result
in distress to the population, who have already suffered
enough. . . ." Ampudia then asked to leave the city with all
of his men and equipment.

Taylor summarily rejected the request. "Unconditional
surrender," Taylor said, constituted the only terms available.
Ampudia requested a personal conference, a meeting which
resulted in an armistice commission composed of officers
from both sides. Worth, Henderson and Davis represented
Taylor.

A nine-paragraph document resulted. The Mexicans
would be allowed to leave Monterrey with their small arms,
and an artillery battery with 20 rounds. Within seven days,
all Mexican troops must be withdrawn behind Riconada
Pass, between Monterrey and Saltillo, and neither side
would resume fighting for at least eight weeks, unless the re-
spective governments ordered otherwise. Ample notice
would be given the other in that case.

Considering the fact that Ampudia had been beaten to his knees, these were magnanimous surrender terms. Taylor explained later that further fighting would have been inflicted on civilians, and since the United States government had negotiated to the bitter end and Ampudia assured him that Santa Anna wanted peace, he believed the terms were humane and justified.

"It is not unknown to the United States government," Taylor said, "that I had the very best reasons for believing that statement of General Ampudia to be true. . . ."

Considering Taylor's command included 6,645 men in attacking Monterrey, his losses were moderate—142 dead and 364 wounded.

The armistice was signed on September 24, 1846, and General Ampudia marched out of Monterrey at the head of his troops on the next day. The American regimental band played "Yankee Doodle," and a 28-gun salute was fired. The American flag was hoisted over all official buildings in Monterrey.

For the moment he no longer faced an enemy, but Taylor was now occupying the hot seat of being fired on from the rear—Washington—although he wouldn't know it for some time because of the miserable mail service.

". . . These armistice terms were liberal," Taylor admitted in a letter to Dr. Wood, "but not considered too much so by all reflecting men belonging to the army here especially considering our situation; besides it was thought it would be judicious to act with magnimity toward a prostrate foe, particularly as the President of the United States had offered to settle all difference between the two countries by negotiation and the Mexican commander stating that said propositions he had no doubt would be favorable met by his government as there was a general wish for peace on the part of the nation. . . ."

President Polk was enraged when he read the terms of the

armistice agreement, and said in his diary: ". . . In agreeing to this armistice, Gen. Taylor violated his express orders and I regret that I can't approve his course. He had the enemy in his power and should have taken them prisoners . . . pushing on without further delay into the country, if the force at his command justified it. . . ."

Publicly, though, President Polk said: "Our troops fought well, though with some loss of officers and men," a comment which damned Taylor with faint praise. Polk was sensitively aware of the public upsurge for Taylor as a presidential candidate. Scott, who had now reassumed command of all land operations because of Polk's lack of confidence in Taylor and the fact that an invasion would be made through Vera Cruz rather than the interior, classified the campaign as "three glorious days." Not even the large casualty list could dampen public enthusiasm for Taylor's personal courage and his unbroken string of victories. Taylor had fought three battles and won three battles. How much better could a general do?

"I did not then, nor do I believe now we could have made the enemy surrender at discretion," Col. Jeff Davis observed about the disputed armistice terms agreement. "The town was untenable while the main fort remained in enemy hands. We could only hope to carry this fort by storm after heavy loss of our army. When all of this had been achieved, what more could we have had gained then by capitulation?"

Lieutenant Meade concurred. In writing to his wife, he said: ". . . For my part, I approve of Gen. Taylor's course. They were still strong in town, having at least 3,000 men and twenty pieces of artillery costing an immense sacrifice to subdue them. . . . Our volunteer forces were beginning to be disorganized. The regulars were crippled almost to inefficiency. . . ."

In view of the divided opinion in both public and military quarters about the justice of Taylor's armistice terms, it was with some misgivings that President Polk called an official Cabinet meeting with a view to condemnation of the armistice agreement. But the Cabinet rubber-stamped Polk's opinions, and a letter was drafted for Taylor which hedged the issue other than saying that it had to be resolved at once.

". . . Notwithstanding the three glorious days at Monterrey," General Scott wrote to Sen. John J. Crittenden, who was Taylor's firm friend, "the terms of capitulation came very near to causing Taylor to be recalled, his standing with the public alone saved him. . . ."

While many American newspapers were beginning to call the conflict with Mexico "Mr. Polk's War," pointing out that the President had miscalculated when he thought it would be possible to "swallow up Mexico at a single mouthful." Taylor was proceeding with his occupation duties in a major Mexican city, and while the furor raged in the United States, he'd had no word about the abrogation of the armistice.

Eleven

THE ARMISTICE

Following the smashing victory at Monterrey, children throughout the United States chanted a brutal doggerel:

> Old Zach's at Monterrey,
> Bring out your Santa Anner;
> For every time we raise a gun,
> Down goes a Mexicanner.

News of the victory touched off new celebrations and excited talk about Taylor's being proposed for president. Medals were struck off, eulogies were written and spoken about Taylor, and toasts were drunk in his honor everywhere.

But no glass of celebration was raised in his honor at the White House. It wasn't entirely because drinking was forbidden by Mrs. Polk. The President, with elections looming large, feared the consequences to the Democratic Party if Taylor continued to draw attention to himself, taking all of the plaudits and leaving the mistakes for the administration. Polk made his first move when he sent orders to rescind the armistice which Taylor made with the Mexicans, and took time to criticize Taylor for his conduct. But it was some time before the dispatches reached Taylor.

Meanwhile, he was consolidating his gains with the occupation of Monterrey. Following the departure of the Mexican troops from the city, Taylor assigned Worth to command the occupation duties, a choice assignment awarded because of the gallant conduct of his men during the campaign. Military morale sagged when the saloons and gambling halls were placed off limits to the troops, all of whom were anxious to relax following the battle. Some of the troops, notably the Texans and Kentuckians, became so obstreperous that Taylor threatened to give them all bad conduct discharges if their conduct didn't improve.

"Shall we ever see the big fandangos in the Halls of the Montezumas?" was the cynical comment of the soldiers. But the discipline was not accepted gracefully, if at all.

"There have been disgraceful brawls and quarrels, to say nothing of drunken frolics," one of Taylor's staff officers wrote. "One captain resigned rather than face trial over several charges. Two others are on trial for fighting about the favors of a low woman."

A priest, Father Rey, and a soldier escort were shot during daylight on the streets of Monterrey.

A 12-year-old boy was used as a target for rifle practice.

Taylor insisted that the men be kept busy drilling, foraging or attending to their weapons, but they always found enough leisure time to cause trouble. Most of the Texans were mustered out, and Taylor publicly thanked them for their patriotism and service but privately admitted that he was glad to see them leave. It was Corpus Christi and Matamoros all over again. No wonder the Mexicans called occupation troops *Godammes*.

Taylor had completed his plans for the advance on Saltillo, which lay 65 miles to the south, when the order to rescind the armistice was received on November 2. Taylor was furious and sent a courier to inform Ampudia of the order and that hostilities would begin forthwith.

"The Old Man is very angry," Dr. Mills said, "and flies about like an old hen with one chicken."

It was with good reason, Lieutenant Meade observed, because Taylor "finds himself called upon to perform impossible things, and has not even control over his own forces." Such was the curse of mixing the army and politics, Meade also said.

Despite his discomfiture and anger, Taylor moved quickly to complete his plans for the advance on Saltillo. General Worth was ordered to alert his troops, while General Butler, who would be the vice-presidential candidate in the next Democratic election, remained in command of Monterrey.

By November 12 Worth was on his way south, and Taylor prepared to follow him. Just then a courier, Maj. R. N. Lane, arrived carrying orders from Washington. Taylor was astonished. He was being ordered to remain in Monterrey. Other troops dispositions were being made and Taylor's command should keep what they had captured and move no farther.

Taylor considered the orders, then continued with his preparations to follow Worth into Saltillo! He refused to have the Washington armchair strategist dictate his strategy and safety. The overt defiance of orders made the break with Polk final and irrevocable, but the crusty old general hadn't acted impetuously or in a moment of pique. Taylor believed that if he had to take the responsibility of command, then he must have the authority which attends it. He added that the Polk administration was conducting a campaign to drain away his authority even while he was fighting the Mexicans. In the light of later disclosures about Polk's diary entries and public statements, Taylor's preception was astute.

President Polk later noted in anger that Taylor had failed "to cooperate with the government in prosecuting the war . . . and he has no sympathy for the administration and cares only for himself."

Taylor expressed his concern in a letter to Dr. Wood: ". . . There is, I hear from high authority, an intrigue going on against me; the object of which is to deprive me of the command; my only sin is want of discretion on the part of politicians in connecting my name as a proper candidate for the next presidential election. . . ."

Taylor's suspicions of a conspiracy were well founded. One of his aides, General Pillow, Polk's ex-partner, was feeding adverse information about the conditions at Monterrey and about Taylor himself to Washington. When Taylor was superceded in command by Scott for the final land conquest of Mexico, Pillow said: "This gives men joy and congratulation. It is my work."

Polk, it was apparent, planned to scuttle Taylor's popularity and when General Scott was reinstated as land commander (a situation about which Taylor knew nothing for some time), orders were sent out detaching various troops from Taylor's command. Of these, Taylor was immediately aware, though they came through Secretary Marcy's office.

Conners was busy ferrying men to Tampico. General Kearny conquered Santa Fe, and was on his way to seize California. General Wool was sent to capture Chihuahua, and Col. Alex Doniphan, the recklessly brave officer, was sent on his incredible march through the wilds of Mexico. Even General Patterson, one of Taylor's staff officers, was withdrawn to occupy Tamaulpais. All orders were designed to dim the sheen of glory worn by the victorious general, Zach Taylor.

". . . While I remain in command of the army against Mexico, and am therefore justly held responsible by the government and the conduct of its operations," Taylor sputtered angrily in a letter to Secretary Marcy, "I must claim the right of organizing all detachments from it, and regulating the time and manner of their service. . . ."

General Scott—who, the President said, was "moved to tears" when he was reappointed to command—made an egregious error from the moment he took control. He wrote Taylor two letters.

One referred to the troops which would be required for military operations elsewhere, and suggested a meeting in Camargo to discuss the matter. As developments became apparent, Taylor studiously avoided the meeting with Scott and other senior officers.

The second letter outlined the future strategy for the entire war, and it fell into enemy hands!

Scott said that Taylor would be held at Monterrey, most of his troops detached and these men used to make the main strike through Vera Cruz toward Mexico City. He gave troop estimates and dates for attacks, along with other vital military intelligence. The letter was given to Lieut. John Richie for delivery. He was ambushed by the Mexicans and the letter intercepted! It was immediately conveyed to Santa Anna. Now the Mexican general knew more about the over-all strategy than Taylor—or anyone, for that matter, since he was aware of Taylor's situation. It could have been a fatal blunder.

Knowing that the Americans were massing for an attack on Vera Cruz and wouldn't be moving any men to help Taylor, Santa Anna gathered his men to mount an assault against Taylor. It was too late for him to blunt the occupation of Saltillo, which had been accomplished without opposition, but Santa Anna believed he could now crush Taylor's army in the north. Then he would turn and repel the planned invasion at Vera Cruz. It was an enviable position for a military man to find himself in.

Taylor moved on to take Victoria, a small village not far from Saltillo. He sent word to General Wool to hold his troops in readiness for future moves. Wool, who had been sent to occupy Chihuahua, was stalled in the area because of the miserable roads which would not accommodate his heavy vehicles. Wool's command would soon be consolidated with Taylor's army, which was further depleted by more detachments for operations elsewhere.

On both sides of the border, the generals were being given ample public advice about the future conduct of the war. "Crush Taylor in northern Mexico", the Mexican press urged. At the same time, the American public demonstrated its displeasure with Polk and his treatment of Taylor. The off-year elections went against the Democrats, and the Whigs obtained a seven-vote majority in the House, 117 to 110. That change of political fortunes heartened Taylor considerably, because he had now decided to accept the presidential nomination if it became available to him. He had written his friend Senator Crittenden to that effect. Taylor admitted that he had considered resigning his commission in view of the shabby treatment which he had been accorded, but he was now determined to complete the demands of the command, no matter what happened. His temper boiled when he received another letter from Scott which said: ". . . I must ask you to abandon Saltillo and make no detachments, except for reconnaisances and immediate defense much beyond Monterrey. . . ."

Lightheartedly, Taylor observed that he didn't consider Scott's letter anything more than friendly advice, and he immediately pushed on farther southward. He moved through La Angostura ("the narrows") and established a forward field headquarters at the Hacienda Agua Nueva, 17 miles from Saltillo along the road to San Luis Potosí, where Santa Anna was gathering his storm troops.

Taylor's strategy was to fight Santa Anna by gradually withdrawing as conditions dictated. He chose the advance post with that in mind, believing that he could stretch Santa Anna's supply lines to the breaking point as he fought a rear-guard action. Taylor did not want to give Santa Anna the opportunity to fight for Saltillo or Monterrey, because the Mexican general might be able to arouse the sympathy of the Mexican residents to help him, and Taylor certainly did not want to fight on two fronts. Besides, either city would provide Santa Anna with an excellent base of operations if he was able to penetrate them.

At the same time, Taylor chose a second line of defense. He was conservative about his ability to defeat Santa Anna. His intelligence reports indicated Santa Anna was leading 20,000 soldiers. To assure a defense in depth, Taylor established a battle line at the Hacienda Buena Vista, leaving some supplies and men at Augua Nueva. Taylor realized he would need some men and supplies, but the strategy dictated the move.

Buena Vista was a collection of clay-roofed buildings which were perched beside the Saltillo road. There was a narrow defile at Buena Vista which was webbed on both sides with other deep ravines studded with cactus and Spanish bayonets. These natural defenses would squeeze the enemy into small numbers in close quarters if they tried to push through. The road, too, was abutted by sheer cliffs about 80 feet high, which flattened out to a plateau and rose gently toward the mountains farther east. Taylor considered Buena Vista perfect for defense, and it had the additional asset of being situated where Santa Anna would have to complete an arduous, thirsty march across 300 miles of desert to reach it. Taylor's battle plan seemed secure, and the morale of his men was high. Taylor exuded confidence in his attitude and on the evening of February 21, 1847, he stepped aboard Old Whitey and rode into Saltillo to check on men and supplies there.

"Let the Mexicans come," Taylor told a *New York Tribune* correspondent, "and damned if they don't go back a good deal faster that they came. . . ."

Taylor deployed his men and weapons carefully at Buena Vista, placing great reliance on his artillery batteries. One was commanded by Captain Bragg, the other by Capt. John Washington. Their cannons were placed athwart the road and on both flanks to enfilade the approach. Rifle companies

and Dragoons were placed near the head of the ravines
ready to swoop down on any Mexican units bold enough to
try a flanking movement through that difficult area. Taylor
withdrew other units about five miles to the rear, where
they would be held in reserve.

Col. Archibald Yell was in command of the 479 Arkansas
Volunteers who had been left at Agua Nueva. They would
receive the first thrust of the expected attack. General Wool
was in nominal command of the forces stationed at Buena
Vista. Taylor believed all was ready even though he had but
4,759 men in his army to face an attack from 20,000 Mexicans led by Santa Anna.

Tension mounted as the hours dragged on without sight
of the enemy; but he was on his way. Santa Anna had
moved rapidly northward despite heat, lack of water and
chilling nights as they moved through the higher passes.
Santa Anna was riding in his gold-leafed coach, which was
drawn by eight white mules. He was dressed in one of his
most ornate uniforms, its coat embossed with 15 pounds of
gold lace.

The march was demanding on both men and animals, but
Santa Anna was unrelenting and didn't slacken the pace. His
forces had thinned to about 15,000 by the time he reached
Agua Nueva, owing to the rigors of the forced march. Santa
Anna himself led the 2,500 cavalrymen which launched the
assault against Colonel Yell's position. But he found that
Yell had evacuated the position during the night, leaving
nothing more than a few supplies, which were burning.

Santa Anna was anxious to press the fight. Because of
Yell's retreat and the burning supplies, Santa Anna believed
that Taylor wasn't planning to make a determined stand.
The Mexicans pushed on toward Taylor's troops. He was so
confident that the Mexicans were masters of the situation
that Santa Anna sent troops in a flanking movement to trap
any retreating Americans. These Mexicans, led by Colonel

Mino, were instructed to call upon residents in Saltillo to fall upon the beaten Americans and capture or kill those they could. It was what Taylor had anticipated Santa Anna would try.

Always the schemer, Santa Anna sent an aide, his surgeon general, to Taylor under a flag of truce, urging the American commander in the name of humanity to surrender because he was surrounded and any resistance was hopeless.

". . . But as you deserve consideration and particular esteem, I wish to save you from a catastrophe . . . under the full assurances that you will be treated with consideration. . . . To this end you will be granted an hour's time to make up your mind. . . ."

Taylor, using a forage cap as a desk, hurriedly wrote: "Sir: In reply to your note of this date summons men to surrender my forces at discretion, I beg to leave to say that I decline acceding to your request. With high respect, I am, sir, Z. Taylor. . . ."

When Santa Anna's representative continued to explain that there were thousands of crack Mexican troops facing the pitifully few Americans, Taylor snapped that he didn't care if there were 50,000 Mexicans out there.

"General Taylor never surrenders," he said with finality. It was a happy choice of words in such a situation. They became a battle cry and a political slogan later on.

Santa Anna's men had their own fighting slogan: "Liberty or Death"—not original, but stirring.

Bitterly cold winds swept through the pass that night, and both Mexican and American shivered and suffered with the chill. The armies were so close together that reveille for one woke the other as well. The Americans watched the enemy celebrating Mass. Taylor tensed. As soon as the services were completed, he knew the battle would be joined. Though he felt no personal fear, Taylor had tasted battle

many times and always tensed when he was offered another
dish of it. Orders were snapped to inspect weapons and
that mounts were securely saddled and that cannonballs,
powder and swabs were all in proper places. In honor of the
day, February 22, the password was "To the Memory of
George Washington."

General Taylor, riding Old Whitey as usual, sat in full
view just behind the center of the main skirmish line. He
was not far from either Bragg's or Washington's batteries,
where the men stood ready with lighted matches to touch
off the first barrage.

General Blanco's division opened the attack. The men
were sent directly up the Saltillo road directly into the cannons. Matches dipped to touch holes, and the cannons
roared and belched shot. The Mexicans staggered and fell,
but they continued the advance into the jaws of death. Another barrage and the ranks were further winnowed. Santa
Anna then committed General Pacheo's division a few at a
time, piecemeal, and they were chewed up as they moved
into the fight. Both of the main assault forces slowed, then
fell back. Santa Anna sent his cavalrymen into the flanking
ravines, all of which were guarded by both rifle companies
and cannons.

"There lies the path to victory," Santa Anna shouted, wav-
ing his jeweled sword. His horse had just been shot out from
under him, and he was now riding an aide's pony. He threw
Ampudia's infantry to force a foothold on Taylor's eastern
defensive line, where they might attain a shelf and provide
a path to Buena Vista, where an attack could be made from
the rear. The mounting fury and force of the Mexican attack
made Taylor's men withdraw a distance. Taylor, still direct-
ing the battle from Old Whitey, whistled up Bragg's artillery, and elements of the Kentucky Volunteers. Their added
fire power slowed the Mexican advance, then began to push

them back down the slope from where they had started. Taylor, sweeping the field with his glasses, gave orders to his officers.

"Give them a little more grape, Bragg," Taylor yelled at his artillery officer as the Mexicans pressed toward the battery. It was remarkable that Taylor didn't fall with a sniper's bullet in his heart, because his white horse and unusual uniform made him a select target.

The first day's battle ended with the lines little changed, though Santa Anna had gained some ground. Casualties were heavy on both sides, but perhaps no more than expected for a close-quarter combat—perhaps even less. Taylor realized it would be a do-or-die attempt by Santa Anna the next day. Taylor regrouped his forces, adding strength to flanks where he thought Santa Anna would try to turn the Americans. He was right.

At daylight the massed infantry attack began. They came on so strongly and so fast that Taylor's men had little time to reload between waves of grim, advancing Mexicans. Santa Anna pressed the attack with 4,000 of his best lancers and aimed a charge at the right center of Taylor's lines. Bugles sounded and pennants waved. The leader of each Mexican regiment rode a white pony to guide their men as they approached the American lines. Taylor's men stood fast without firing a shot until the Mexicans were within 70 feet. Then a fusillade erupted, and the Mexicans dropped like toppling dominoes. The cannons, loaded with chain shot, snaked through the ranks, biting and slicing. The Mexican bugles sounded retreat—but not soon enough for hundreds. The battlefield was littered with the maimed, the dying and the dead. But Santa Anna was equal to the disastrous situation. Defeat could be turned into victory through device.

A messenger, bearing a flag of truce, was sent to General Wool's field headquarters, who ordered firing halted as the courier rode up. Nearby were Mexicans who had been surrounded by the Americans, and both sides stood still while the courier delivered his message. But no sooner had the messenger met with Wool than the Mexican bugles sounded and the surrounded Mexicans dashed for freedom, making good their escape through surprise before the Americans could fire a shot.

"What is General Taylor going to do about that?" Santa Anna chortled. Taylor was speechless with anger, having lost the advantage through the trick.

Santa Anna took the offensive, slamming 12,000 men against the Illinois and Kentucky Volunteers. Taylor's men recoiled with the sheer force of the attack, and Bragg's guns were moved forward to rain cannister down on the Mexicans.

"Our shot went crashing through them, and our shells likewise, opening for themselves a bloody circle wherever they exploded," the artillery officers said.

Unable to face the withering fire, the Mexicans retreated slowly. Not even the Napoleon of the West, his sword flashing as he nudged the sides of his pony with his peg-leg, was able to stem the disorganized retreat.

One minor unit gained the rear of Taylor's men near Buena Vista. Lieut. William Shover spotted them and sallied out with two field guns, which frightened off the Mexicans, who fled into the mountains.

In midafternoon, a heavy rain began to fall, soaking the soldiers but providing them with cover so they could recover their wounded comrades, who were taken to field stations at Buena Vista or Saltillo. Extra rations were issued and tight security guards posted, and Taylor then conferred with staff officers. All were gloomy and somewhat apprehensive about the next day's battle. Battle casualties were reported at 673 for the Americans and an estimated 1,800 for

the Mexicans. Even so, Taylor stated, they would stand their
ground no matter what Santa Anna threw against them.
There could be no retreat.

The night passed without incident, and the men were
pulled awake to meet the expected attack. Outpost guards
yelled jubilantly: "They've gone. The Mexicans have left."

General Wool confirmed the withdrawal, then told Taylor.
The two men embraced, tears rolling down their cheeks.
Three days of rest were immediately granted all of the men.
Taylor wrote a general order: "The General would express
his obligations to the officers and men engaged for the cordial support which they rendered throughout the action. It
will be his highest pride to bring to the notice of the Government the conspicuous gallantry of different officers and
men whose unwavering steadiness more than once saved the
fortunes of the day. He would also express his high satisfaction with the conduct of the small command left to Saltillo."

Taylor made passing reference to the few men who had
deserted and had gone over to the Red Battalion. He said
these men should expunge their dishonor by returning to the
American forces for discipline.

General Scott sent word of the great satisfaction that he
felt with the "great and glorious victory." Even Washington
was forced to grudgingly give commendation to Taylor.
Wrote Marcy: "The general joy which the intelligence of
this success of arms had spread through the land is mingled
with regret it has been obtained at so great a price, that so
many heroic men have fallen in that sanguinary conflict."

Taylor established order in the area. The smashing victory
caused great concern in Mexico City. Many consider the
battle at Buena Vista climactic in the American conquest of
Mexico because it struck such terror into the hearts of Mexican troops that they never fought so valiantly again.

Santa Anna later said that Taylor was beaten on at least

three occasions during the battle, but was too brave to know it.

There had been a great deal of national concern for the safety of Taylor's little army because of the hazards he faced due to the stripping of his forces by Polk and General Scott. As late as March long after the battle had been fought; the *New Orleans Gazette* commented: ". . . We are waiting in painful suspense further tiding from the gallant General Taylor. God grant that the many rumors in circulation are without foundation. . . ."

Taylor's name was on every mind, every tongue. And there was a great outburst of public joy when the good news of Taylor's safety and victory at Buena Vista finally reached Washington. Both President Polk and Secretary Marcy made wry faces at the public response to the news. Polk began to wonder if his idea to appoint two Whig generals, so that they would divide the glories between them and leave him as the center attention, was going to work. Taylor looked like a shoo-in for the presidency if he sought it during the next election.

Old Rough and Ready was supremely confident of his military abilities and was becoming even more confident that he would be able to gain the greater prize, the presidency, when he returned to the United States. With that thought, and with the battle done, Taylor patted Old Whitey and rode back to Monterrey, where he would sit out the rest of the war against Mexico. But he was an old soldier who was determined not to fade away in the backwaters of politics and war.

He realized that the armistice of Monterrey had been a decisive turning point in his career.

Twelve

POLITICS

As intelligence reports filtered into military headquarters, Taylor, Wool and the other officers were increasingly impressed with the magnitude of the victory over Santa Anna at Buena Vista. Tattered remnants of the Mexico legions were in full flight. Behind them weapons, ammunition and supplies were scattered over the landscape, along with disabled men and animals abandoned to whatever fate dealt them. Even so, a sense of jubilation eluded Taylor.

"The great loss on both sides," he wrote to his brother Joe, "has deprived me of everything like pleasure." He was bitter of having been stripped of men at such a crucial time. "If Scott had let me have 500 or 1,000 regular Inf., the Mexican Army would have been completely broken down, & the whole of their artillery and baggage taken or destroyed."

Taylor had reason to be embittered. When all were discovered, casualties proved higher than the first estimate. There were 746 dead and wounded. Colonels Yell and McKee and Lieut. Col. Henry Clay, Jr., son of his old friend Henry Clay, were dead. His son-in-law, Col. Jeff Davis, was grievously wounded, although he did recover fully.

Taylor was utterly tired of war and of killing, even more so when he reassembled his thoughts in writing to the grieving parents of Henry Clay. His letter said, in part: ". . . A

138

grateful people will do justice to the memory of those who fell on that fateful day. But I may be permitted to express the bereavement which I feel in the loss of valued friends. To your son I felt bound by the strongest ties of private regard; and when I miss his familiar face and those of McKee and Yell, I can say with truth, that I feel no exultation in our success. . . . Z. Taylor, March 1."

In paying honor to the dead and wounded, Taylor didn't overlook praise for the troops who had survived, and he was extremely generous in his official reports for the conduct and bravery of his officers and enlisted men, while taking none for himself.

Taylor, however, had risked more than anyone else, in a sense. He had openly disobeyed orders by moving southward from Monterrey, and his defiance would have been severely dealt with if the battle had been lost. Even so, President Polk was outspoken in his rage with Taylor. Polk placed the blame for the heavy casualties directly on his shoulders. The President said it was only the army's inordinate bravery that saved Taylor from court-martial.

Taylor pointed out that Santa Anna had to be met and stopped at some point, or else the entire northern campaign would have been without military meaning. Taylor had been able to select the best possible battlefield. It was fought entirely on Taylor's terms, and the victory restrained the Mexican general from initiating any mischief among the Mexican residents of any town.

And the public back in the States sided heartily with their hero-general. The issue strengthened the presidential boom for Taylor.

Taylor realized as fully as anyone that the armistice at Monterrey had been a turning point in his military career, and that he would have no further opportunity to command military operations because of it. He applied for a six months' leave, then settled back in Monterrey to write letters of both personal and political nature. Though his Cypress Grove plantation badly needed attention, Taylor had now been bitten by the political bug. Some of his heightened interest may have stemmed from a desire to defeat Polk, if he should be a candidate.

Taylor was held in high regard by politicians. "I regard him as one of the noblest specimens of human nature I ever saw," one Virginia officer wrote about Taylor. "He is perfectly unaffected by his brilliant successes, plain and unassuming in his manners, mild and affable in his disposition, and kind and courteous in his demeanor. . . ." Letters such as that one—and there were hundreds of them, sent to relatives and friends at home—produced a great impact on the public and became the basis for what was known as "The Taylor Tradition."

His furlough was granted, and on November 26 Taylor boarded the *Monmouth*, bound for New Orleans. Aboard with him were many of the sick and wounded soldiers—so many, in fact, that there were insufficient accommodations. Taylor gave up his quarters and spent the trip sleeping on a mattress pulled near the ship's boilers.

Four days later, Taylor made a triumphal return to the United States. Though he had been born in Virginia and raised in Kentucky, he was now considered a resident and an adopted son of Louisiana. It was from there that he would launch his political career.

". . . Discharges of cannon and display of [the *Monmouth's*] flags announced that she was bearing home to Louisiana her distinguished citizen," a report in the *New Orleans Picayune* stated. ". . . Every ship and every steamboat from the bar to the pilot station mustered its hands and cheered a welcome. . . ."

Even more important to Taylor was the fact that his wife, daughter Betty and son-in-law Dr. Wood were all there to greet him. They had been apart for two years. But they were reunited on December 3 in a lavish tribute unequaled up to that time in the history of colorful New Orleans.

Ships hoisted their colors, and buildings were gaily festooned with bunting. Taylor rode Old Whitey along a parade route lined with throngs of people, perhaps as many as 40,000. Poor Old Whitey. His tail was nearly pulled from its roots by souvenir seekers who wanted a remembrance of their hero, General Taylor. The horse was nearly plucked bald before a guard was assigned to restrain the hair pullers. The Mayor of New Orleans presented Taylor with the keys to the city and Taylor replied modestly, placing most of the credit for his victories on the bravery of his men. At that juncture, Walt Whitman, the poet, described Taylor as "a jovial, old, rather stout, plain man, with a wrinkled and dark yellow face." But his admirers cared little about appearance, and the welcome, one account said, "made the very welkin ring."

The explosive, enthusiastic celebration lasted two days before Taylor managed to board the *Missouri* with his family and get away to Baton Rouge, where another vibrant welcome awaited him. On the river trip, people lined the banks to wave at him. There was no doubt that Taylor had a firm grip on the public's affection; and the politicians knew it. At times, there were tears welling up in Taylor's eyes. Never in his 63 years had he ever imagined that such a tribute would be paid him.

Taylor made a few modest speeches, but retreated with his family to their Spanish Cottage, in which they had lived previously, as soon as possible. The Taylors spent the next 13 months there. His military career was virtually at an end, but another, national politics, was beginning.

Taylor had some time to mend his own personal fortunes. The two plantations that he owned were losing money and required close personal attention. One was leased out and was later sold for a loss. The other Cypress Grove, comprising about 2,000 acres, was located on the banks of the Mississippi not far from Natchez. Taylor purchased it for about $100,000, mostly inherited money, believing it would be a retirement place when he left the army. At that time, he had no vision of fighting in Mexico, or being a presidential candidate. On his plantation, Taylor had 125 Negro slaves, a figure which placed him among the most substantial slaveholders. Taylor, with long experience on his father's estates, was a thrifty, prudent farmer, but the plantation never did well. In the years when the cotton crop was good, the price was low. When the price was up, the river overflowed and ruined his harvest. He usually referred to the venture as "my unfortunate plantation."

While he might have been a failure as a plantation owner, Thurlow Weed considered Taylor a winner politically, especially in light of the homecoming receptions. Weed had also been responsible for the nomination of Gen. William Henry Harrison, the ninth President. Weed warned Taylor not to write any letters which might be published and compromise his position, or at least be misconstrued. Taylor played it in the best American political tradition when he was approached by representatives of the Native American Party seeking Taylor as their candidate.

While he appreciated the honor of being asked, Taylor said, he was not an active candidate just at that time. "I could not," he said, "while the country is at war and while my duty calls me to take part in the operations against the enemy, acknowledge any ambitions beyond that of bestowing all of my best exertions toward obtaining an adjustment of our difficulties with Mexico."

Taylor remained reluctant, even as the political ground swell mounted. In response to an editorial in the Cincinnati Signal, Taylor remarked:

". . . In no case can I permit myself to be a candidate of any party, or yield myself to party schemes. . . ." In effect,

Taylor was suggesting a public draft, noting that his nomination, if it came, should be the "spontaneous action of free will of the Nation at large."

One Kentuckian, obviously more enthusiastic than educated, shouted: "I tell ye General Taylor is going to be elected by spontaneous combustion."

Mrs. Taylor vigorously opposed his trifling in national politics, maintaining that they had earned a rest and the remaining years together. Taylor himself had some reservations about the wisdom of getting involved in politics, however intriguing. Uppermost in his mind was the scurilous campaign which had been conducted against Andy Jackson, including remarks which were directed at his wife.

Though Taylor was publicly reluctant about the nomination, there were others seeking the honor. Henry Clay, who was given an excellent chance of grabbing the nomination, sought it desperately. General Scott harbored similar ambitions, though it seemed likely that if a war hero was chosen, it would be Old Rough and Ready. Daniel Webster, John McLean and Thomas Corwin all actively sought the nomination.

Party schism and competition wasn't confined to the Whigs. President Polk announced that he didn't want another term. Though he later softened the statement, it was too late. No mention was made of him at the convention. Active candidates included General Lewis Cass, a hero of the 1812 War, John C. Calhoun, Silas Wright, George M. Dallas, James Buchanan and two of Taylor's generals, Worth and Butler.

When it became apparent that Taylor was a candidate, critics carped that he had no grasp of national issues and was an inept statesman. But his letters and public statements showed clearly that Taylor had an astute understanding of national problems and that he held firm opinions about them. Opposition was strident because Taylor was a slaveowner, an issue which was becoming increasingly important. Taylor publicly approved of the Ordinance of 1787, written to stay the spread of slavery in the southwestern and western areas. He showed that he did not flinch from endorsement of the law even though it alienated many of his staunch Southern supporters. It might have been a bid for political support from the North, but he demonstrated unswerving fairness in questions about slavery. Taylor acted according to his own lights, rather than those of political expediency.

Because of the war costs, which were about $22,000,000, Taylor wanted higher tariffs to raise revenue. He also advocated the application of all funds derived from the sale of public lands to reduce the national debt and for the reduction of costs of government itself. Moreover, Taylor followed the policy of Tyler. He wanted to give the national treasury a chance rather than resort to a national centralized banking system, which was again being urged.

Taylor was adamant in his opinions about the use of the Presidential veto, a position which drew support from both partisans and enemies.

"No president should hesitate to veto any law which conflicts with provisions of the Constitution, but on matters of expediency great forbearance should be used and only after the most mature consideration," Taylor said. Taylor qualified the statement to included instances of veto to protect Congress from unreasonable demands made by the electorate.

The bulk of his statements were published in *The Signal* and caused some controversy. At first, he seemed to lose support because of his forthright stand, but as the opinions were reconsidered and the inherent honesty of the statements showed through, even his opposition realized they were confronted with a man who wasn't afraid to state his mind though his opinions might not be immediately popular. Many newspapers acclaimed his opposition to the spoils system—awarding political jobs to relatives or political hangers-on. As his campaign gained momentum, Taylor stated that he would not abandon his fight for the nomination even to favor Clay. In turn, Clay said he thought Taylor was naïve and presumptuous for even becoming involved in politics.

Abraham Lincoln, then a Whig representative from Illinois, organized a Taylor-for-President Club during the winter of 1847–48, and two slaveowning Georgians, Robert Toombs and Alex Stephens, came forward to endorse him. Strange bedfellows, made possible through political accommodations, were not unknown even then.

Part of Taylor's preconvention campaigning was done through letters addressed to Capt. John S. Allison, who had married Taylor's sister Emily. The letters were later published in the *New Orleans Picayune* where they gained a large circulation. Among Taylor's policy statements were that "the personal opinion of the individual who may happen to occupy the executive chair ought not to control Congress upon questions of Domestic policy; nor ought his opinion & objections to be interposed when questions of Constitutional power have been settled by the various Departments of government and acquiesced in by the people."

There were many other points that Taylor included in the so-called Allison letters, all of which were favorably received by most of the public.

Still there were dissensions. Rallies for Taylor were interrupted by gangs of New York toughs, known as the Dead Rabbits and the Bowery Boys.

To curb these disturbances, Toombs hired Capt. Isaiah Rynders, a New York hoodlum himself, to keep order at the meetings. Rynders' men circulated through the audiences, surreptitiously making chalk marks on the backs of known troublemakers. With the first outbreak of trouble, Rynders'

men pitched the opposition out into the street within minutes because they had all been spotted. After the iron discipline of Rynder's men had been imposed a few times, the
Taylor rallies had little trouble.

Curiously, both slaveholders and abolitionists approved of
Taylor, but one Southerner said he didn't want to support a
president who might deprive him of the one hundred slaves
and other property.

". . . I have the honor to inform you that I have too been
all my life frugal and industrious," Taylor wrote in reply,
"and that the fruits of my labor thereof are mainly invested
in slaves, of whom I own *three hundred*. . . ."

It was an unarguable reply, as even Thurlow Weed admitted.

When Weed felt that Taylor had the nomination secured,
he approached Daniel Webster about taking the second
place on the ticket as vice-presidential candidate. Webster
had almost decided to accept when their meeting was interrupted by Fletcher Webster, who flatly stated that his father's own presidential campaign was going so well that no
attention should be paid to Weed's suggestion. Webster
then refused, unwittingly depriving himself of eventual succession to the presidency on Taylor's death in office. He did,
however, support Taylor following his nomination.

After all deals and manueverings had been accomplished,
both parties, the Whigs and the Democrats, scheduled their
meetings. The Democrats met on May 22, 1848, in the Universalist Church of Baltimore, with Andrew Stephenson of
Virginia presiding.

From the time of the first gavel banging, it appeared that
Lewis Cass, Governor of Michigan, had the edge, and on the
fourth ballot he received the necessary two-thirds of the 171
votes required for nomination. Gen. William O. Butler, one
of Taylor's aides, was unanimously elected for the vice-presi-
dency on the third ballot. It seemed like a strong ticket, but

the antislavery Democrats and the Barnburners were enraged with the nomination. (The Barnburners were a radical splinter group of abolitionists who were given the derisive name in reference to the man who foolishly burned his barn to get rid of the rats.)

J. M. Morehead presided when the Whigs convened on June 7 in the Museum Building of Philadelphia. Like the Democrats, delegates tried to start a debate on the hotly bruited Wilmot Proviso, which prohibited any slavery in territory acquired from Mexico. But the issue was not publicly discussed before the convention. Though Taylor's stand on the Proviso was not clear before the election, as President he said it was the source of sectional conflict and ignored the Proviso entirely in the case of California, believing that the choice of slavery should be a sovereign decision of the individual states.

Taylor was a front runner from the first convention ballot, with Clay second and Scott a weak third. On the fourth ballot, Taylor got some votes from each of the 30 states represented in the convention and he was nominated. It was then made unanimous. Millard Fillmore of New York was chosen as the vice-presidential candidate on the second ballot. Fillmore was a lawyer and had served in the New York legislature. The convention cheered lustily at the final choice of candidates.

". . . Taylor's nomination takes the Locos on the blind side," Abe Lincoln wrote a friend following the convention. "It turns the war thunder against them. The war to them is now the gallows of Haman, which they built for us, and on which they are doomed to be hanged themselves. . . . One unmistakeable sign is that all odds and ends are with us— the Barnburners, Native Americans, Tyler men, disappointed office-seeking Locofocoes, and the Lord knows what all. . . ."

The Locofocoes were radical democrats and obtained

their curious name when the gas fixtures were mysteriously extinguished to prevent the count of a standing vote. The hall was then illuminated with candles lit with matches called "locofocoes," a name which was then applied to this segment of the Democratic Party.

Lincoln's estimate of the political strength behind Taylor was not entirely accurate, because the Locofocoes, the Barn-burners and the Hunkers, who favored slavery, all coalesced into the Free Soil Party and convened during August in Buffalo, New York. Martin Van Buren (the eighth President) and Charles F. Adams were selected as a third-party presidential ticket. But when they received no electoral votes at all, Van Buren retired to private life.

During all of these doings, Taylor was in Louisiana and didn't know that he had been named the presidential candidate. It was some time before he was officially informed because he refused the letter from the Whig Party as it lacked sufficient postage. Candidate or not, Taylor wasn't going to be careless with his money.

150　　OLD ROUGH AND READY

Thirteen

THE SUCCESSFUL CAMPAIGN

Abe Lincoln, Thurlow Weed and other leading Whigs realized that the upcoming presidential campaign would be hard-fought because Cass was a skilled, politically dangerous opponent. Lincoln took to the hustings for Taylor, chiding the Democrats as only Lincoln could. Referring to the Democrats' attempt to claim the attributes of Jackson as their own, Lincoln observed: ". . . A fellow once advertised that he had made a discovery by which he could make a new man out of an old one and still have enough stuff left over to make a yellow dog. Just such a discovery has General Jackson's popularity been to you Democrats. You not only twice made a president out of it, but you have enough left to make Presidents out of several comparatively small men since, and it is your chief reliance now to make still another. . . ."

Lincoln was a vigorous campaigner and unsheathed another weapon when he accused Cass of having drawn $1,500 of public funds to pay office rent and a clerk's wage while he was Governor of the Michigan Territory. Neither of these costs existed, Lincoln claimed, and demanded that Cass publicly explain. It was ignored. The *Baltimore American* commended Lincoln on his adroit campaigning for Taylor,

149

referring to Abe as "a very able, acute, uncouth, honest, upright man, and a tremendous wag withal. . . ."

The campaign had been under way for some time, and Taylor remained blissfully unaware that he had been nominated. His nomination had been spearheaded by Weed, and no one actually asked Taylor for his formal permission because it was believed that he still might refuse to run in view of his earlier reluctance.

But when the nomination had been accomplished, a telegram of notification was sent to Memphis, then forwarded on to New Orleans. Taylor didn't consider the wire to be official notification, though he didn't say why. Taylor asked Jeff Davis where he could contact John Morehead, who had been in charge of the convention, to inquire if a letter had been addressed to him. The mystery was finally solved when Taylor remembered he had refused a letter which was delivered with postage due. Because of his tendency to be careful with a dollar, Taylor was among the last to know that he was a candidate for the President of the United States.

It was a curious campaign. The convention, after choosing their candidates, proposed no platform, on the rather tenuous theory that the North and South would never agree anyway. Such issues as the extension of slavery, tariffs and national banking were all left to the individual interpretation of Taylor and other speakers, not all of whom agreed!

"Speaking is going on from the principal stands and from a dozen stumps," newspapers reported. "Fireworks, squibs and crackers are in full operation."

Taylor believed it was undignified for a presidential candidate to travel about the nation attending political rallies and asking for votes. Despite the fact that he differed with the Polk administration on nearly every national policy, he refrained from taking issue with Polk on any viable issue. Taylor continued with his military duties as commander of the western department of the army, living at his headquarters in Baton Rouge. He wrote a few letters which were published and stated his views, but the campaign was generally listless.

Truman Smith was the national campaign manager for the Whig Party. He was a congressman from Connecticut and had been active in Whig Party affairs for many years. Though he had favored Clay at the convention, he became an enthusiastic advocate for Taylor. Smith was called by the Democrats the "principal schemer, spokesman and general circular-letter writer for the Whig Party." The charges were partially true. It was revealed that Smith blandly used his Congressional franking privilege to send out thousands of Whig brochures, speeches and political literature, all of which were written to advance Taylor's cause.

Smith, in unblushing enthusiasm, compared Taylor favorably with George Washington, cheering Taylor's heroism as he enumerated the military victories and recalled the smell of blood and gun powder from Buena Vista and Monterrey.

Slavery was the most important issue during the 1848 election. Cass stated only that the matter should be settled in the new territories on a local level—squatter sovereignty. And that was all he had to say about the vital issue.

Taylor was equally cautious about the slavery issue, though perhaps wiser. He stated that his attitude would be to abide by the will of Congress in acting on such matters. A presidential veto would be used only in such cases which he believed to be "cases of clear violation of the Constitution, or manifest haste and want of consideration by Congress."

Taylor gained popularity as the campaign progressed. His positions allowed the Northerners moral justification to vote for him, since they didn't believe he would veto the Wilmot Proviso if it was ever enacted. The Southerners could also find reason to vote for him partly because he was a slaveowner and had written his son-in-law Joff Davis: ". . . This Wilmot Proviso should have never been agitated. [It] was gotten up with no other object but to array the North against the South, & I much fear its injurious effects before it is finally disposed of; but I hope for the best. . . ."

Throughout the entire campaign Taylor went no farther than Louisiana and a small section of Mississippi. He wrote other letters to Captain Allison which outlined his views. The torchlight parades on his behalf increased, and with the public demonstrations, disturbances and sometimes riots erupted over the candidates and issues. During a parade which passed in front of the Old Rough & Ready Political Club in New Orleans, a Taylor supporter taunted the marching Democrats. One man thrust a torch in another's face, and he drew a pistol and began firing wildly into the crowd. The Democrats then burned the clubhouse, and the parade continued.

As the election day drew near, Whig strategists forecast that Taylor would win 163 of the 290 possible electoral votes, an estimate which proved to be exactly correct. Cass received 127.

For the first time in the history of the United States, all presidential electors were selected at the same time, on Tuesday, November 7, 1848. The only exception was South Carolina, where the legislators made the final choices, but the election and decision was made on the same date.

Because of the completion of the magnetic telegraph, the news of the election was gathered rapidly. By Friday of election week, it was apparent that Taylor had won. He received 1,360,099 votes. Cass got 1,220,544, Van Buren 291,-263.

Though the election had been relatively close, Taylor's vote came from all sections. He won in 15 states, of which eight were southern and seven northern.

Taylor received the news that he was elected president calmly. One observed that he seemed disappointed, and would have probably preferred to retire from the army and become a planter. But duty to Taylor always came before the fulfillment of personal desires, and it was with that attitude he went forward to face the enormous problems which always confronted Presidents.

President Polk was disconsolate with the news of Taylor's election, stating that he believed that Taylor was wholly unqualified for the high office. ". . . He will rely on designing men and will reverse, so far as the Executive can reverse, the whole policy of my administration," Polk wailed.

General Taylor continued with his military duties, preparing to leave for Washington as soon as he could. He was plagued by a constant stream of visitors, job seekers and well-wishers. Taylor received as many as he could, despite his limited time, but finally his temper snapped. He made it clear that he had other important matters to occupy his time and none but the most vital would be entertained.

One duty was a personal matter. He gave his daughter Betty in marriage to his aide Col. William "Perfect" Bliss. The General admitted that he couldn't have been more pleased with her choice, even though he had opposed the marriage of Knox to Jeff Davis. Bliss would continue to stand by the General's side in the years ahead at the White House.

With the induction into office scheduled for March, the Taylors began preparations to move in January. Taylor refused an offer of free transportation to Washington, an offer which he didn't consider ethical to accept because of his position. Mrs. Taylor, whose health had been affected during the years of traipsing after her husband and raising six children, expressed her unhappiness with the move to Washington. She loved the Baton Rouge area and their home along the river. Margaret Mackall Smith Taylor believed it was now time to rest and relax and was unhappy in being denied that choice. To spare her public exposure and the crush of celebrants, Taylor arranged that she, along with

Colonel and Mrs. Bliss, would travel to Washington on a route different from the one he would use.

In preparation for the formalities, Taylor ordered two new custom-styled suits. He was amused to discover that the tailor had been besieged by people who wanted to stuff the pockets with letters, requests for jobs and other solicitations so they would come to the attention of the President-elect. The tailor was astute enough to charge a small fee for collecting these blandishments and giving them to General Taylor, who immediately discarded all of them. But it was a part of his baptism in the ways of office holders. He was often awakened at six o'clock by visitors who wanted his attention for even the most trivial matters.

By mid-January of 1849, Taylor had completed arrangements to move and had resigned his commission to the army, a post he had held for 40 years. To his neighbors and other friends in the Baton Rouge area Taylor said, during an informal farewell: ". . . Had I consulted my own wishes, I should have much preferred to remain among you and retain my present office in the Army. . . . I fear that I am not qualified to discharge the great and important duties ahead of me, but I assure you that I shall do my best without fear or favor. . . ."

The trip to Washington was an abomination for Taylor. He was pushed, kissed, petted and saluted with both cannon and whiskey. He eschewed lionization as he always had, but he was a public figure now and found that he had no privacy. Worse still, in a dimly lighted passageway on the river steamer, Taylor tripped over some baggage and was painfully injured in one arm and in his side. Then the boat on which he was riding hit a snag, and all passengers had to be ferried ashore. In the skiff which carried Taylor, one man was taken in wine and his antic conduct nearly upset the boat.

"Sit down, you drunken fool," Taylor snapped, his voice

carrying the same timbre of command which made troops move. The man sat down, looking sheepish, and the passage was made without further difficulty. Taylor had probably saved his and the others' lives by his ability to demand obedience.

On the way, Taylor had considered choices of Cabinet members. Crittenden was asked to become Secretary of State, but he declined and suggested John M. Clayton, who eagerly accepted the assignment.

Because of delays occasioned by various celebrations, levees and balls given in his honor, it was 8:30 P.M. February 23, the first anniversary of the battle at Buena Vista, before Taylor arrived in Washington. There he was greeted by an enthusiastic throng of about 3,000 people. He was escorted through the cheering, excited crowd to the Willard Hotel, where his wife, daughter and son-in-law waited to greet him.

Taylor was obviously happy to be reunited with his family, and remained in seclusion for the first weekend without being besieged by visitors. Taylor's injuries still pained him, and there was work to be done on his inaugural address—a matter which he had given little thought to in the rush of other events since election.

President Polk, cold, aloof and still unhappy about his successor, gave no official notice to Taylor's arrival. Polk noted in his diary that it was protocol that the President-elect made the first social move, and Polk was abiding by that. By Monday after his arrival, Taylor, accompanied by his wife, Jeff Davis and Clayton, called at the White House at about midday. The President came down to receive them.

". . . I received General Taylor with courtesy and cordiality," President Polk recorded in his diary. "He remained about 20 or 30 minutes. I invited him to dine with me Thursday next. He replied he would so if his health permitted it."

President and Mrs. Polk gave their formal affair in the White House during his final week in office. The affair which bade farewell to officials in Washington also welcomed President-elect and Mrs. Taylor. It was a huge affair, with all of the important political, military and social figures attending—All except Taylor himself, though his immediate family was present.

The next night, March 1, there was a private dinner at the White House which honored both Taylor and Fillmore, along with the other VIPs. The dinner was finely "gotten up in Julian's best style," and no politics were served with the cuisine.

President Polk completed his official duties, signing those bills which still required his signature, the most important of which was the enabling legislation to provide governments for both New Mexico and California. There were still some lingering thoughts that the much-discussed Wilmot Proviso be tacked on to these measures, but at the last minute the House amended the bills to provide that the laws of Mexico, which had abolished slavery long before, would prevail in all new territories until Congress should act to amend them. Since the Mexican laws contained the stricture against slavery and would remain operative, there was a great deal of excitement among the Congressmen from the southern states.

"It was a moment of high responsibility," President Polk said referring to the bills, "Perhaps the highest in my official term."

A curious circumstance marked the start of Taylor's administration. The designated day for the inauguration, March 4, fell on a Sunday, and the formal proceedings were put over until the next day. Since Polk's term technically expired on March 3 and Taylor didn't take the presidential oath of office until March 5, the President-for-a-Day myth has grown apace with the lore of American Presidents. With

that lapse of official time, it has been contended that Senator
David R. Atchison, president pro tempore of the Senate, was
actually President by line of succession during the unoccu-
pied twenty-four hours. The issue was not raised at the time
because there were no matters which required official presidential attention, but it has become a matter of historical cu-
riosity since then.

One hundred federal marshals gathered in front of the
Willard Hotel on inauguration day, March 5, to escort the
President-elect to take the oath. A raw wind whistled
through the streets; the flags and pennants snapped in response. Taylor stepped into an open carriage which was
drawn by four gray horses. With him were two aides, Major
W. W. Seaton and Senator Robert Winthrop, though only
the latter rode with Taylor. The horses were whipped up,
and they pulled the carriage to the Irving Hotel, where President Polk had taken quarters and awaited his successor.
Polk stepped into the carriage, and the men shook hands.
Taylor sat on the right, Polk on the left. They both waved
and nodded to the crowds which lined Pennsylvania Ave-
nue. In spite of strenuous efforts by peace officers to control
the crowds, admirers moved into the street and blocked the
carriage. It took more than an hour to reach the summit of
Capitol Hill.

Even as they smiled and nodded to the throngs, Taylor
and Polk talked politics and the future of the nation. Most
of the snatched discussions centered around the California
and Oregon situation. Polk considered Taylor's opinions
"alarming," and his other diary entries were equally conde-
scending and spiteful. "Taylor," Polk said, was "no doubt a
well-meaning old man," but of "very ordinary capacity."

Polk added: "Taylor is, however, uneducated, exceedingly
ignorant of public affairs, and, I should judge of ordinary capacity. He will be in the hands of others and must rely
wholly upon his Cabinet to administer the Government."

It was high noon when Taylor, Polk and Winthrop entered the Senate chamber. An improvised wooden platform had been constructed at the east portico for the ceremonies. The order of performance differed from modern times. The oath of office was not administered until after the inaugural address had been delivered.

Taylor accepted the task of speaking to the 20,000 people who had gathered to witness the solemn event. Taylor's speech was, perhaps, remarkable for its brevity and lack of content. It was more a document of welcome and gratitude and an expression of his personal philosophy than a forward-looking statement setting the course of a growing nation.

". . . With such aids [men of character being selected for his Cabinet], and an honest purpose to do what is right," Taylor said, "I hope to execute diligently, impartially and for the best interests of the country, the manifold duties devolving upon me. In the discharge of these duties my guide will be the Constitution I swear this day to preserve, protect and defend.

"For the interpretation of that instrument I shall look to the decisions of the tribunals established by its authority and to the practice of the government under the earliest Presidents, who had so large a part in its formation. To the example of those illustrious patriots I shall always refer with deference, and especially to his example who won the title of the Father of his Country. . . . I this day renew the declarations I have heretofore made, and proclaim my fixed determination to maintain, to the extent of my ability the Government in its original purity, and to adopt, as the basis of public policy, those great Republican doctrines which constitute the strength of our national existence. . . ."

Aware of the emergence of the Second Republic in France, Taylor observed that he agreed with Washington's policies in staying free of entangling alliances with foreign governments. ". . . It is our interest, no less than our duty, to remain strictly neutral; while our geographical position, the genius of our institutions and our people, the advancing spirit of civilization, and above all, the dictates of religion direct us to the cultivation of peaceful and friendly relations with all other powers. . . ."

Taylor made oblique references to the policy of patronage, adding a promise that appointments within his administration would be made in accord with the honesty and capacity of the person involved, implying that party labels wouldn't assure a job. Taylor would be reminded of that statement when Democrats were dismissed on a wholesale basis.

President Taylor made only one veiled reference to slavery when he said: ". . . I shall look with confidence to the enlightened patriotism of Congress to adopt such measures of conciliation as may harmonize conflicting interests, and then to perpetuate the Union, which should be the paramount object of our hopes and affections. . . ."

Following his remarks, Taylor then took the oath, which was administered by Chief Justice Roger B. Taney, and turned to receive congratulations.

"I hope, sir, the country may be prosperous under your administration," ex-President Polk said as he shook Taylor's hand. Later they left the White House together, with Polk returning to the Irving Hotel, where he sat down and entered a few observations. In referring to Taylor's delivery of the address, Polk wrote: ". . . Pulling down the spectacles which slept in his hair, Taylor read his speech in a very low voice and very badly as to his pronunciation and manner. . . ."

Offsetting Polk's snide remarks, the *National Intelligencer* remarked that Taylor delivered his speech "in a remarkably distinct voice, and many parts of it were enunciated with a full and clear emphasis. . . . There was frequent cheering, whether or not those farther away could hear what was being said. . . ."

The *Boston Atlas* commented: ". . . The first thing which will strike the reader is the brevity of the document, and the next, the admirable manner in which he has expressed his views upon the duties of the Chief Magistrate. . . . We have compared it favorably with those of Washington and the earlier presidents. . . ."

The Taylor administration took office on a note of controversy. The merit of what he accomplished during the next 18 months is still a matter of spirited debate.

Fourteen

THE WHITE HOUSE

President Taylor didn't get along well with the Congress from the outset, even though his appointments for Cabinet posts were immediately confirmed.

Taylor's Cabinet members included Thomas Ewing, Ohio —Department of the Interior (which President Polk had created during the waning days of his administration); John M. Clayton, Delaware—State; William M. Meredith, Penn. —Treasury; George W. Crawford, Georgia—War; William B. Preston, Virginia—Navy; Jacob Collamer, Vermont— Postmaster General; and Reverdy Johnson, Maryland—Attorney General. All were Whigs and all were more or less professional politicians, with the exception of Crawford.

There were editorial sighs of dismay when the members were announced. ". . . The weakest Cabinet in twenty years," the *New Hampshire Patriot* said. The *Kentucky Yeoman* agreed by saying, "The Cabinet will be far inferior to the one with which Polk retired. . . ." And "Taylor cannot be congratulated on the strength of his Cabinet," the *Memphis Appeal* stated.

Editors friendly to Taylor said many good things, however. With Taylor in office, the *Nashville Banner* said, "The country has a guarantee of ability and patriotism. And the *New York Herald* thought the Cabinet was well organized as to balance, and "composed of intelligent and respectable men. . . ." And the *Louisville Courier,* which was extremely proud of its home-town son, said editorially: ". . . We have never seen a happier co-minglement of usefulness and greatness than in President Taylor's Cabinet."

It became a matter of what newspaper one read to assess Taylor's judgment and ability. But it seemed to be an era of good feelings, at least in comparison with the gloom and austerity of the Polk administration. There was an aura of hospitality and friendliness shown by President Taylor and his daughter Betty, who took the place of Mrs. Taylor as hostess, as the latter's health and disposition didn't permit her to be the First Lady in the formal sense. Betty—plump, vivacious, young and intelligent—had assumed the duties from the first party held in the White House. She dressed without ostentation but in excellent taste, often wearing a rose in her hair and always carrying herself with "the artlessness of a rustic belle and the grace of a duchess."

President Taylor came in for a spate of criticism, especially from the Democrats, when he allowed his Cabinet members to make their own appointments and dismissals. Democratic job decapitations began on a wholesale scale. Three thousand people were removed from the Post Office Department within the first few weeks, and critics screamed that the Government was in the hands of the Cabinet and not the elected President. "Taylor has but one vote of the seven," the critics said.

Even loyal Abe Lincoln wasn't able to manage an appointment for a friend in the general land office, and wrote to Taylor complaining that he believed that the President was relying too heavily on members of his Cabinet. But a staunchly loyal Whig newspaper observed that it was foolish to believe that a man of Taylor's disposition, a man used to commanding and winning the loyalty and support of his troops, would change simply because he had now become

President. Taylor was still in command, the *St. Louis Republican* said, and he would act when it was necessary. There was no need to overreact.

". . . I did not think it wise or just to kick away the ladder by which I ascended to the Presidency," Taylor wrote to a friend. ". . . Officers are just as necessary in politics as they are to discipline and efficiency in an army. Rotation in office, provided good men are appointed, is a sound republican doctrine. . . ."

Taylor said that he believed his Cabinet members to be "harmonious, honorable, patriotic, talented, hard-working and of irreproachable private character." And Taylor, believing that, allowed the Cabinet to act in line with their own best judgment. When Taylor felt he should intercede, he did, and brooked no argument. Nor was any recourse possible. Taylor became disenchanted with his Cabinet, especially with Clayton, who was the rallying point for cleavage within the Taylor administration and the Whig Party generally.

Patronage, always a touchy subject because it often oiled the wheels on which a political band wagon moved, became the disruptive issue. The Southerners claimed that the Northerners were being given too many of the choice jobs simply because Thurlow Weed, a northerner, had been Taylor's first sponsor. Besides, the smoldering issue of slavery continued to flare up as a peripheral part of every controversy. Even though Taylor was a slaveowner, he had come under the influence of the antislavery faction, some of his critics claimed. This criticism lost Taylor support from Toombs and other influential Whigs from the South.

Senator William H. Seward of New York was permitted to sit in on the Cabinet meeting on a status almost equal with those who carried the rank of a Cabinet officer. Perhaps Seward had even more. He had access to the President and to Thurlow Weed and seemed able to obtain favors which were denied others. Taylor alienated many formerly friendly Democrats who had supported him in the belief he would treat partisans fairly, and they now believed Taylor was little more than a Party President.

Secretary of State Clayton, a brilliant lawyer and a skillful politician, became a bone of contention in both national and international affairs. Clayton was a man of eloquence, but was sadly lacking in tact, patience and understanding, all traits necessary to the successful execution of affairs of state. Clayton was supremely confident—arrogant, some said. "I will give you leave to hand me off like an old acorn if I don't bring out the glorious old man's administration in its foreign policies without cause for complaint even from his enemies."

It was a high goal, but unobtainable by Clayton. He immediately became involved in a messy dispute with French Ambassador William Tell Poussin, who filed a small claim for damages in connection with goods lost as a result of the Mexican War. Clayton was offended by Poussin's attitude and publicly said so, a nondiplomatic move which alienated the French and laid the basis for a second dispute which followed not long afterwards. Though Taylor was not directly involved in the situation, his lack of action in settling the matter reflected on his position as "chief magistrate."

A United States naval vessel, the *Iris*, rescued the French ship *Eugenie* from a reef near Vera Cruz. The American commander, Edward Carpenter, filed a claim for salvage, a move which infuriated the already sensitive French Ambassador Poussin. Before the matter had been resolved, Poussin was recalled, and the new American ambassador to France was snubbed by the French Foreign Minister Alexis de Tocqueville. Taylor was expected to apologize for the conduct of the naval officer, an expectation which Taylor summarily scuttled. Diplomatic relations were strained, and it seemed that a war with France might ensue. American newspapers, especially those of Whig persuasion, printed belligerent editorials urging American firmness in the situation. Reason finally prevailed when, at the last moment, Louis Napoleon, the president of the French Republic and later its Emperor, said that he was "not ashamed to make the first advance." The matter was then settled without much difficulty because it had been a matter of form rather than real substance. The ambassadors were exchanged and associations resumed much as before.

Taylor, not Clayton, proved to be the strong hand in the dispute, and Napoleon implied that the tension was resolved because he didn't relish the thought of the manner with which Taylor would deal with France in forthcoming messages to Congress. President Taylor's firmness and courage, the Frenchman said, had been the deciding factor in obtaining peace, not at the price of national honor.

President Taylor's courage was shown in one way with the French, but in quite another way later on.

". . . I consider our neutrality laws and particularly our treaty obligations as perhaps the most important duty that can demand the attention and action of our Executive," Old Rough and Ready stated in an earlier campaign statement. That expression became the keystone of Taylor's foreign policy.

Following the settlement of the Oregon question with Great Britain, there was some international concern that expansionist-minded Americans might undertake filibustering expeditions into Canada to carve out another empire there, or at least add to the territory of the United States. Already there had been paramilitary adventures into Mexico, Cuba and South America with varying success, and there was no reason to doubt that Canada would be overlooked. The British consul, John F. Crampton, approached Taylor about the administration's attitude in the event of a filibuster into Canada. Taylor assured the Englishman that American troops would be sent at once to put down any such disturbance.

No filibusters erupted, probably because of Taylor's firm statement.

President Taylor also fell heir to a dispute which had been started during the Polk regime. Germany was at war with Denmark and had purchased an American vessel, the *United States*, which was to be converted into a fighting ship. Polk had authorized the use of the Brooklyn Navy Yard to accommodate the reconversion, but Taylor stopped it. He believed the use of the shipyard by a foreign power to be used against a friendly nation was a breach of his neutrality policy.

Work on the ship was halted, and Taylor obtained assurances from the German government that the vessel would not commit any act of war against a nation at peace with the United States. To ensure that the performance would be as agreed, the ship was released under a surety bond set at twice the value of the ship and possible cargo. Fortunately, hostilities were concluded before any test of the bond was made.

Taylor's patience in dealing with foreign policy matters was tested time and again. Cuba was the center of the next controversy. Many believed that Cuba would ultimately become a possession of the United States.

"We must have Cuba," James Buchanan said.

"North America will spread out," a fiesty Southern editor wrote. "They will encroach again and again on their neighbors. . . ."

Many Cuban exiles were living in New York and in New Orleans. They were excited by the leadership of Narciso Lopez, who wanted to throw off the Spanish yoke which had been laid on the neck of Cuba. A Cuban junta, financed with $30,000 sent from Havana, was formed to recruit and propagandize the cause. With Lopez was Col. G. W. White, a veteran of the Mexican War, who was in charge of recruiting while Lopez obtained supplies and ships to provide for the invaders. In Baltimore, enlistments were taken with the soldiers promised seven dollars per month, with the promise of $1,000 to be paid at the end of the first year of service.

Ships were obtained and outfitted and the invasion begun. American naval vessels were sent after them to prevent a landing. The landing was partially successful, because Lopez managed to get ashore with some men and burn a few buildings. Several of the commandoes were captured by the Cubans, and their execution seemed certain. Taylor then took up the cause of the underdogs and interceded for the prisoners. Taylor stated that execution of the men would be considered an act of war by the United States. The Queen of Spain then pardoned all of the prisoners as "new proof of friendship for the United States."

For a man who had never been faced with problems of international scope, President Taylor was proving to be an extremely bold, forceful President who dared anyone to challenge the vigor and might of the United States.

Taylor dared to inform Spain that transfer of Cuba to any other world power would be a signal for immediate war. The French were also warned against establishing any protectorate in the West Indies, or any attempt to control the Hawaiian Islands by any means. Implementing his obvious interest in foreign affairs, Taylor ordered Clayton to make studies of the trade potential with the Far East. These studies resulted in a detailed plan for an expedition to Japan which was later orchestrated by Commodore Matthew C. Perry, opening that country to foreign trade.

Taylor's aggressive policy also resulted in the Clayton-Bulwer Treaty, which provided for freedom of movement by both the United States and Great Britain in connection with any canal across the isthmus in Central America. It was an extremely farsighted agreement. That treaty included a statement that neither nation would "colonize, annex or fortify any part of the ancient territory of Guatemala, embrac-

ing Nicaragua, Costa Rica, Honduras and indeed, the whole
of the Mosquito Coast," over which Great Britain held a protectorate. The agreement was signed April 19, 1850, and
cleared the way for what later became the Panama Canal,
though it took the Hay-Plaunceforte Treaty to define the details of the sovereignty involved.

Democrats complained that the Clayton-Bulwer Treaty
made for entangling alliances and the encroachment of a foreign power into the American sphere of influence in defiance
of the Monroe Doctrine and Taylor's policy statements. But
despite the grumbling, the treaty was approved by the Senate in July of 1850.

Whatever else the critics might say of the Taylor administration, the Clayton-Bulwer Treaty was a giant stride toward making the United States a world power in the real
sense of the term.

Intersticed with these other matters was the desperate revolt of the Hungarians, who were trying to free themselves
from Austrian rule. Taylor was extremely sensitive to such
struggles and wanted to be the first to recognize the new nation if the rebellion was successful. Taylor's stand caught the
public imagination, and there were mass meetings to con-
demn the oppressors.

But Russia provided aid to Austria, and the revolt was put
down. Taylor probably expressed the feelings of all America
when he said: ". . . The oppressed in every land will here
find the same protection that we ourselves enjoy. Here your
rights, and liberties, and religion will be respected and
maintained." It was later disclosed that Taylor had sent a
delegate, Dudley Mann, to be on hand if the rebellion was
successful.

Taylor provoked more criticism because of that sub rosa
move. Many claimed that the United States was becoming
involved in affairs which were of no vital concern to the best
interests of the United States.

Taylor might have agreed privately that he had risked a political venture, but he was quick to demonstrate that the United States, though a young nation, was proud, bold and not afraid to get involved in struggles for freedom anywhere in the world.

It was President Taylor's bold, decisive manner in guiding foreign affairs which marked the successful conduct of the nation's external policy during his brief administration.

Fifteen

END OF A CAREER

Political party lines and alliances were sundered when Congress convened for its official 31st session December 3, 1849. Present were 112 Democrats, 105 Whigs and 13 Free Soilers, with the latter actually holding the balance of power. Though the heated debates seemingly centered on the selection of a Speaker, the pervading specter of the slavery issue hung over the House like a shroud.

". . . I look upon slavery as one of the compromises of the Constitution," said William J. Brown, an Indiana Congressman who had been elected Speaker on the 40th ballot. "I will stand by that institution, and sustain it, as guaranteed by the Constitution of the United States." He emphasized that his constituency would stand with him on that interpretation.

The industrial revolution which was occurring at about the same time had a subtle chemistry in it which encouraged slavery. There had been a huge emigration into the United States, and factories were flourishing in the Northern states. To keep looms humming, the mills spewing out more products, the Southern states needed to expand cotton production, an economic demand which made the South even more dependent upon one crop. As a result, the demand for cotton and the expansion of the cotton lands increased the need for slaves. Many justified slavery by pointing to the fact that their servitude was considered more humane than the manner in which the immigrants were treated when they worked for a few cents an hour, under the worst possible working conditions. The situation became a two-edged argument for retention of slaves and emphasized the value of the slaves, which was estimated at $1.5 billion.

The slaves lived "like princes" when compared with the "wage slaves" of the factories in both the United States and England, according to a story in the proslavery *New York Herald*.

President Taylor made no public statement, since there was no cause for it. He simply repeated his determination to abide by the Constitution and exercise his veto accordingly. Though Taylor didn't take the lead in shaping public opinion, it was, he said, because he believed that the slavery issue would resolve itself.

After all, the world was moving so fast that the slavery issue might be forgotten in the welter of other national affairs. The world was considered so sophisticated that the head of the U.S. Patent Office announced that he wished to resign because he "felt that the limit of human invention had been reached and there would be no further need for his services."

This was during the era when the safety pin had just been invented, when few homes boasted any running water or indoor plumbing, when bathtubs were still being taxed in several states and when interior light was still being provided by candles or whale-oil lamps.

Taylor wanted an overhaul of the postal system to bring the rate down to five cents an ounce for letters sent any distance. Correspondence up to that time was an indulgence of the rich or of the Congressmen, with their franking privilege.

But President Taylor's first annual message to Congress

dealt with more serious problems, including the ever-present slavery issue.

". . . Sixty years have elapsed since the establishment of this Government, and the Congress of the United States again assembles to legislate for an empire of freemen. The predictions of evil prophets, who formerly pretended to foretell the downfall of our institutions, are now remembered only to be derided, and the United States at this moment present to the world the most stable and permanent Government on earth."

While the President rambled on about pedestrian matters during most of the message, there was an electric shock in Congress when he said: ". . . With a view to maintaining the harmony and tranquillity so dear to us all, we should abstain from the introduction of those exciting topics of a sectional character which have hitherto produced painful apprehensions in the public mind; and I repeat a solemn warning of the first and most illustrious of my predecessors against furnishing any ground for characterizing parties by geographical discriminations. . . ."

In full content, the President's statement clearly indicated that the issue of slavery should be skirted in public debate or made a prerequisite of admission as a state. Taylor was obviously a firm believer in both individual and state rights. ". . . The executive has authority to recommend (not dictate) measures to Congress," President Taylor said.

In a private letter to Jeff Davis about his own personal rights and those of several states, Taylor on August 14, 1847, had written: ". . . The moment the abolitionists go beyond the point where resistance becomes right and proper, let the South act promptly, boldly and decisively with arms in their hands, if necessary, as the Union in that case will be blown to atoms, or will be no longer worth preserving. . . ."

Over and over again, Taylor stressed the dignity of man and the sanctity of personal rights, and his belief in the Constitution as the final statement on those things.

Some, including Jeff Davis, believed that the structure of the United States government might change radically within a few years because the trend seemed to be toward allowing states admission to the Union, slave or free.

There were extended arguments in Congress and other public forums about slavery. One of the major results of this continued public attention was a piece of legislation submitted by the so-called Committee of Thirteen, which had been created to sum and try to resolve all of the issues incident to slavery. The Committee was composed of six Democrats and seven Whigs. Of these, seven represented slave states, and six were from free states. Clay was chairman. The document they submitted was a catch-all and lumped all of the pros and cons from all shades of opinion in hope of getting a far-ranging bill through Congress. There was something in it for everyone. Taylor dubbed it "The Omnibus Bill," a name which stuck. After a great deal of polishing, it was finally passed and became known as the Compromise of 1850, though it was actually five pieces of legislation. The Compromise dealt with the fugitive slave situation; the prohibition of slavery in the District of Columbia; the admission of California as a state; settlement of the Texas boundary dispute; and the admission of Utah and New Mexico as territories, but with no stricture about slavery.

The American press was almost unanimously against the bill, calling it "humbug" and a measure which was "sure to create dissension." President Taylor, too, had unconcealed contempt for the Compromise, which didn't actually become law until after his death. Taylor believed that the Compromise included elements which were patently unconstitutional and a jumble of so many other things that it would do little more than to inflame partisan emotions in various sections of the nation.

"Disunion is treason," Taylor said, and he publicly promised that he would personally see that traitors were accorded punishment they deserved.

The Compromise, with its Fugitive Slave Law sections that became the basis for *Uncle Tom's Cabin*, was also the initial schism which led to the dissolution of the Whig Party. The Compromise, while it may have stayed the horrors of the Civil War temporarily, offended both pro and con slavery factions. Taylor's opinions and oppositions were ignored.

". . . The Compromise of 1850 was an attempt to place slavery beyond the pale of practical political issues," historian William Starr Myers wrote. "Taylor, who developed into a president of strength and ability and even of statesman-like qualities, has never received adequate recognition for the stand he took for the Union, and the policy of settling matters a step at a time, but settling them, rather than of attempting to settle everything at once—and really settling nothing at all. . . ."

During Taylor's tenure the tension over the Compromise never diminished. The situation heated up when Texas tried to take control of New Mexico, and the prospects for an open, armed conflict appeared ominously near. The War Secretary said that he would refuse to sign an order for the movement of federal troops to strengthen the military forces in New Mexico, and Taylor replied that if such a move became imperative, "then I will sign it myself."

Alex Stephens, who had been an enthusiastic Taylor advocate, was violently opposed to his attitude.

". . . The first federal gun," Stephens warned, "that shall be fired against the people of Texas without the full authority of law will be the signal for the freemen from Delaware to the Rio Grande to rally to the rescue. . . ."

Toombs supported Stephens in his confrontation with the President, and both men urged Crawford to rescind his refusal to order troops into New Mexico. There was some muttering about an impeachment proceeding against Taylor, and when he was warned about the incipient political rebellion, one friend said:

". . . Southern officers will refuse to obey your orders if you send troops against Texas. . . ."

"Then," President Taylor said, "I will command the army in person, and any man who is taken in treason against the Union, I will hang. . . ."

Fortunately none of these issues reached the flash point where all of the inflammatory statements would have to be fulfilled, but the situation was extremely serious and acrimonious. Taylor stuck to his guns, as he always did, and never signed the bill, nor did he visibly retreat from his stated position.

President Taylor was deeply wounded emotionally by the continuing attacks on his character and abilities. He found some comfort in solitary rides on Old Whitey through wooded areas not far from the White House. Old Whitey, Taylor's faithful companion for so many years, was allowed to pasture on the White House lawn.

When Taylor couldn't spare the time for rides, he usually took walks in the early morning. He often wore a dark suit which fitted loosely on his dumpy frame, and a silk hat which was pushed jauntily to the back of his head. Taylor talked with anyone who bothered to approach him, often at the expense of relaxation for himself.

While debates raged in Congress, Taylor took a brief political excursion to sample public opinion. The junket was interrupted when he fell ill with fever, probably a recurrence of the illness which dated from his military service.

President Taylor found that the East Room of the White House had been redecorated during his brief absence, and even fitted out with gas jets for lighting and heating. The President was pleased too with the new carpeting, he said, which made the White House more homelike.

Mrs. Taylor, though she took no part in the official social functions of the President's calendar, did make a home for Zach. She also entertained close friends in her own rooms and did a modest amount of unofficial entertaining of her own. Mrs. Jeff Davis said of her:

". . . I always found the most pleasant part of my visit to the White House to be passed in Mrs. Taylor's bright, pretty room where the invalid, full of interest in the passing show in which she had not the strength to take her part, talked most agreeably and kindly to the many friends admitted to her presence. She always appeared at the family dinner, to which a few friends were unceremoniously bidden, of which many charming ones were given during General Taylor's administration, ably bore her share in the conversations at the table. . . ."

Other friends spoke well of Mrs. Taylor's intelligence and ability to make interesting conversation, though rumors continued to circulate about Washington that something secret must be wrong with her. It was inconceivable to members of the gregarious, social-climbing Washington hostesses that any woman would not want the power and social acclaim which naturally accrued to the wife of the President.

Similar to the vicious rumors which circulated about President Jackson's wife, Rachel, was the gossip that Margaret Taylor was locked up in an out-of-the-way room where she sat mindlessly puffing on a corncob pipe, perhaps dreaming of the rustic, nomadic life they had followed during her husband's 40 years in the army.

These speculations were, of course, unfounded, but it was another burden of office which the General had to bear unnecessarily. His daughter Betty presided at the social functions and did very well indeed: ". . . She had that *je ne sais quoi*, that knowledge of how to be just cordial enough, and yet not too cordial," one social arbiter commented. "Never has the White House had a gentler, sweeter mistress. . . ."

While the official functions required formal dinners and similar functions, President Taylor preferred the small, inti-

mate dinners at which he could entertain his close friends, or others he may have considered it expedient to entertain. Reaction to the President himself was almost as varied as his guests. All agreed the President always dressed casually, his clothes often rumpled and usually a trifle out of fashion. One guest said President Taylor was "polite, cordial and talkative. . . . I confess he is rather more polished and entertaining a gentleman with more ease, than I expected."

Another visitor differed, saying that the President was an "outrageously ugly, uncultivated, uninformed man . . ."

All agreed that the White House cuisine was excellent. The President, though he had been used to eating Army rations or whatever was available, had a taste for Louisiana cooking, Creole style. He was very fond of oysters, and the Opelousas Oyster Gumbo was his favorite dish. Even more exotic was the Coon and Squirrel Deep Dish Pie, which was a delight to those from the South and a surprise to those who weren't and unused to the Creole style of cooking.

President Taylor had been in office only little more than a year when the Galphin Claim scandal erupted. He was fully prepared to cope with external threats, war, Democrats or other issues. But he was wounded deeply when people he trusted, such as members of his Cabinet, betrayed his trust and became involved in a nasty public affair.

The Galphin Claim started 75 years earlier. At that time, the Creek and Cherokee Indians had been supplied with $50,000 worth of goods in exchange for certain lands. Heirs of the Indians claimed the transaction had been faulty and demanded $191,352 in accumulated interest. Attorney General Reverdy Johnson approved the claim, though he had been the attorney of record for the claimants. War Secretary Crawford also approved, and Treasury Secretary Meredith paid it. Taylor's enemies seized on the payment, maintaining that the Cabinet members were part of a conspiracy, or in-

competents at least. Taylor was held at fault because he had appointed these men and made it possible for such things to happen.

President Taylor was deeply hurt and confused about what should be done. He discussed it with Thurlow Weed, suggesting that the entire Cabinet be dismissed. The innocent members would be given diplomatic posts; the others would be out of government. Weed vetoed the idea as too drastic. Nothing was decided or done during the meeting held in June of 1850. Time would solve the matter soon enough.

Weed wrote Colonel Bliss after he had talked with the President, pointing out that Taylor's health was failing and he was concerned about it. Weed said the shock of the scandal had a telling effect on Taylor's health. Bliss said he would get Dr. Wood to examine the President, but other matters interfered and he couldn't get to the White House before the President attended the exercises at the Washington Monument on July 4. Once there, the President complained that the heat made him feel giddy, observing that Washington seemed to be hotter than either Mexico or Florida.

". . . The old hero sat in the sun at the Washington Monument during the long spread eagle address by Senator Foote, with a tedious supplementary harangue by George Washington Custis—exposed to the heat for nearly three hours. [The President] had drunk heavily of iced water and returned to the White House weary, fatigued and still complaining of headache and dizziness. . . ."

Upon his return to the White House, President Taylor found a large basket of cherries, and he began to gobble them. As he ate, he drank several large goblets of chilled milk, a combination which was thought to ensure indisposition. Despite the snack, the President said he was hungry when dinner was served. Following the meal, he continued his feast on the cherries, in the face of an admonition from

the White House physician, Dr. Witherspoon, who was a dinner guest that evening.

Before the President was able to dress for the party planned for the evening, he was seized with cramps. Dr. Witherspoon ordered him to bed and, because the illness appeared trifling, no report was made to the public. Nothing was announced for five days, though wild rumors were rampant by then.

On July 9, there was a short statement from Dr. Witherspoon:

"The President is laboring under a bilious, remittent fever, following a serious attack of cholera morbus, and is considered by his physicians seriously ill."

Crowds gathered at the White House, and it seemed that debates were held in hushed tones in the Congress. When the President's fever raged even higher and signs of congestion and failing vital signs appeared, Congress was told the President might not survive the day. Congress adjourned.

That night July 9, 1850, at 10:30, President Taylor died. His final words to his family, his Cabinet and the others who gathered near were: ". . . I am about to die. I expect the summons very soon. I have endeavored to discharge all my official duties faithfully. I regret nothing, but am sorry that I am about to leave my friends. . . ."

Next morning, President Millard Fillmore issued a formal proclamation to Congress: "I have to perform the melancholy duty of announcing to you that it had pleased Almighty God to remove from this life Zachary Taylor, President of the United States. He deceased last evening at the hour of half past ten o'clock, in the midst of his family and surrounded by affectionate friends, calmly and in full possession of all his faculties. . . ." Fillmore then stated that he would take the formal oath of office that day at noon "to enable me to enter on the execution of the office which this event has devolved upon me. . . ."

Bells throughout Washington tolled in slow cadence. Differences in politics were set aside during the time of national grief. Lincoln led the eulogies in the House; Webster did the same in the Senate.

Thousands of saddened Americans viewed the President's body as it lay in state in the East Room of the White House during Friday, July 12, 1850.

". . . I never saw grief, public grief so universal and so profound," William Seward wrote.

Next day the city awoke to the sound of funeral cannon salutes, which continued booming throughout the morning. Gen. Winfield Scott, aboard a spirited horse, led the funeral cortege. He was resplendent in full-dress uniform, with a yellow panache fluttering from his bell-shaped helmet. Elements of the artillery batteries which had fired the first and last shots during Taylor's Mexican campaign moved along in the silent procession. The funeral carriage was pulled by eight white horses, each of the animals led by a Negro garbed in white.

Old Whitey, his saddle empty and his master's boots reversed in the stirrups, walked behind the funeral carriage.

After a brief ceremony, President Zachary Taylor was interred temporarily in the Congressional burial ground. Later, he was removed to the family burial plot on the Beargrass Creek plantation, near the place which Zachary Taylor had loved so much and where he wanted to live out his life.

He had finally come home, once and for all.

SIGNIFICANT DATES IN ZACHARY TAYLOR'S LIFE

1808: Received commission as lieutenant in Army
1810: Appointed captain
1811: In command of Fort Knox
1812: Leads gallant defense of Fort Harrison and given a brevet to major as a result
1815: Resigns from army
1816: Returns to army as major of Third Infantry
1819: Promoted to lieutenant colonel, Fourth Infantry
1822: Builds Fort Jesup
1828: Commands Fort Snelling
1832: Made colonel
1832: Final battle of Black Hawk War at Bad Axe
1837: Brevetted to brigadier general for distinguished service in Okeechobee battle against Seminole Indians
1846: Mexicans cross Rio Grande and clash with scouting party, April 24
1846: May 8, Mexicans defeated at Palo Alto
1846: May 9, Mexicans defeated at Resaca de Palma
1846: Matamoros captured without bloodshed, May 18
1846: Brevetted to major gen. for distinguished service in Mexico, May 28
1846: July 18, received Congressional commendation for courage

1846:   September 25, captures Monterrey after bitter,
        bloody battle
1847:   Defeats Santa Anna at Buena Vista, February 23
1848:   Receives nomination from Whig Party as presi-
        dential candidate
1849:   Resigns from army
1849-1850:   President of the United States

SUGGESTED FURTHER READING

Armstrong, O. K. THE FIFTEEN DECISIVE BAT-
TLES OF THE UNITED STATES. New York: David
McKay Co., 1961.
Cunliffe, Marcus. THE NATION TAKES SHAPE. Chi-
cago: University of Chicago, 1959.
Hamilton, Holman. ZACHARY TAYLOR, SOLDIER
OF THE REPUBLIC. Indianapolis: Bobbs-Merrill,
1941.
Leckie, Robert. THE WARS OF AMERICA. New York:
Harper & Row, 1968.
Merrill, James M. SPURS TO GLORY. Chicago: Rand
McNally, 1966.
Stillman, Richard J. THE U.S. INFANTRY: QUEEN
OF BATTLE. New York: Franklin Watts, 1965.
Wormser, Richard. THE YELLOWLEGS: STORY OF
THE U.S. CAVALRY. Garden City: Doubleday, 1966.

INDEX

185

ABOUT THE AUTHORS

The collaboration of Bob and Jan Young began at the University of California at Los Angeles, where they met as undergraduates and found they shared a common interest in writing. Following their marriage in 1940, they spent most of the next ten years in the newspaper field. In 1950 they turned to free-lance writing, concentrating first on the magazine field. In 1958 they published their first two books for children and now, after numerous other books, consider writing for young people their major interest.

Both are native Californians. Bob was born November 6, 1916 in Chico; attended Sacramento schools, UCLA and graduated from the University of Nevada. Jan was born March 6, 1919 in Lancaster; attended Pt. Loma and South Pasadena public schools and UCLA. They are the parents of four children.